58.

Diana Darke

THE
OTTOMANS

A CULTURAL LEGACY

With 24 illustrations

To the memory of Professor Alan Jones (1933–2021)

Cover: Bold, brightly coloured Ottoman tilework epitomizing the peak of Ottoman craftsmanship and aesthetic sensitivity. The stylized tulip panel from the prayer hall of the Rustem Pasha Mosque (*c.* 1650) in Istanbul. Photo from Kenan Kaya/Alamy Stock Photo.

Title page: Street vendor selling *salep*, a warming winter drink made from wild orchid root, sugar and hot milk. Photo by G. Berggren, part of his 1870s series *Portraits of inhabitants of the Ottoman Empire*. Private Collection. **Page 6:** Genealogical tree of the Ottoman sultans, produced in 1866–67, during the reign of Sultan Abdulaziz. The imagery of the entire dynasty bursting forth from a single tree reflects Osman's visionary dream. Gianni Dagli Orti/Shutterstock. **Page 14:** Photograph of three women – one Muslim, one Jewish and one Bulgarian – from Salonica (Thessalonica), *c.* 1873, illustrating the city's complex make-up. Photograph by Pascal Sébah, from Osman Hamdi Bey and Marie de Launay, *Les costumes populaires de la Turquie.* Library of Congress, Washington, D.C.

First published in the United Kingdom in 2022 by
Thames & Hudson Ltd, 181A High Holborn, London WC1V 7QX

First published in the United States of America in 2022 by
Thames & Hudson Inc., 500 Fifth Avenue, New York, New York 10110

This paperback edition published in 2024
Reprinted 2025

The Ottomans: A Cultural Legacy © 2022 and 2024
Thames & Hudson Ltd, London

Text © 2022 Diana Darke

British Library Cataloguing-in-Publication Data
A catalogue record for this book is available from the British Library

Library of Congress Control Number 2022931876

ISBN 978-0-500-29818-3

Printed and bound in the UK by CPI (UK) Ltd

Be the first to know about our new releases, exclusive content and author events by visiting
thamesandhudson.com
thamesandhudsonusa.com
thamesandhudson.com.au

CONTENTS

Introduction: A Fresh View • 6

INTRODUCTION
A Fresh View

IT IS TIME, a century on from the dismemberment of their empire following the First World War, to look afresh at the Ottomans. They lived in a world very different from our own, yet there is much we can learn from the way they structured their societies, just as there is much to appreciate in how their unique achievements have enriched our lives.

The global context must be understood when we attempt to piece together the Ottomans' legacy – quite a challenge when even modern Turkey, the successor state to the Ottomans, has a love–hate relationship with its Ottoman past. In considering a 600-year empire that straddled Europe, Asia and Africa, and encompassed an enormous diversity of peoples, there will inevitably be both good and bad. Every world empire, not least the British, had its share of lived tragedies.

Equally fallacious is to apply today's lexicon to events of the past. Expressions such as 'the Turkish yoke' and 'multiculturalism' represent two extremes. The first was invoked by 19th-century nationalist paradigms, while the second is loaded with 21st-century overtones that did not exist in Ottoman times. Prejudice is part of the picture, and history is written by the victors, so theirs is the view that inevitably seeps into our consciousness. This book does not seek to pass judgment on the Ottomans one way or the other, or to exonerate them from what were clearly violent acts. Yet it is as if, as a people, they have disappeared. I am struck by the fact that the word 'Ottoman' rarely figures in the index of most guidebooks to Balkan countries; where it does, the reader is referred instead to the entry for 'Turkish domination', perpetuating the narrative of an oppressive rule by a detested alien power. The education systems of most Balkan countries do likewise, ensuring that new generations grow up with the same mindset, since modern European nationalist views based on religion and language necessitate the rejection of all things Ottoman.

Across the provinces of the Arab world that were once under Ottoman rule, opinions on the period are more nuanced. Although Ottoman Turkish was the language of court judgments and was still used by the army and police into the early 20th century, Arabic remained one of the official and literary languages, and Ottoman cultural influence was minimal across the Maghreb. In Tunisia, after French colonialists imposed a protectorate in 1881, local people are said to have scanned the horizon hoping to see Ottoman ships arriving again. In Syria and Egypt, views of the Ottomans wax and wane according to the politics of the day. The Syrian government's view, for example, was broadly positive in the days when Turkey's President Erdoğan and Syria's President Assad used to holiday together. When the two fell out in 2011 after Turkey supported the Syrian opposition, the official school history syllabus was changed to refer not to 'the Ottoman era' but to 'the Ottoman occupation'.

The Ottomans ruled over an area more extensive than the Byzantines, and for a longer period than the Romans. Their empire was in many ways the successor to Byzantium, in the same way that the Byzantine Empire was the successor to Rome. All three empires were based in the Mediterranean and used long-lasting institutions to rule over a diverse assemblage of ethnicities, religions and cultures, therefore representing the very opposite of today's nation-state.

Yet, unlike the Roman and Byzantine empires, whose legacies have been described exhaustively by generations of European historians, the cultural heritage left by the Ottoman Empire has often been neglected, sometimes even wilfully ignored. This has been exacerbated by academics traditionally shying away from such a lengthy time period and such a vast geographical area. Some focus only on the Arab provinces, others only on the Balkans. Some are scholars of Turkish, others of Hellenic or Byzantine Studies. The result is a fragmentation of knowledge. For the sake of the general reader, therefore, my aim here is to venture a broader overview of the Ottomans and their historic influence, covering the fields of commerce, society, religion, science, music, language, literature, cuisine, and home and lifestyle. My approach is thematic, so that I can showcase this enormous diversity, enriched by the book's carefully chosen illustrations.

Putting together the pieces of this Ottoman legacy has proved a challenging and complex puzzle. Like many in the West, I did not realize how 'European' the Ottomans were. I was surprised to learn, for instance, that, when Constantinople was conquered in 1453, it was not by Muslim hordes advancing from the steppes of Asia, but by a mixed Muslim–Christian army already based on the European mainland. For over a century, a quarter of the Ottoman Empire's territory lay within what today is Europe, yet such boundaries as existed in the European mind were never shared by the Ottomans. Even during the second siege of Vienna in 1683, 100,000 Hungarian Christians fought on the Ottoman side, as did thousands of Slavs, Greeks,

Armenians and Transylvanian Protestants, disenchanted with the Catholic fervour of the Habsburgs and the feudal levies of their own aristocrats.[1] That is not to say that either side were angels, of course, but the narrative in which a valiant Christian Europe battles against a despotic Muslim Orient is a Disney version of history. Muslim–Christian collaboration and coexistence were present to an extraordinary degree despite the religious wars of propaganda painted by both sides.

Christian Greeks and Muslim Turks had lived alongside each other in Anatolia for centuries under the Ottomans' Turkic predecessors, the Seljuks. At the height of the Seljuk sultanate in the 13th century, the Christian Greeks outnumbered the Muslim Turks by as many as ten to one, according to the Flemish explorer William of Rubruck, a contemporary observer of the Seljuk state.[2] The historian Warwick Ball tracks how the Turks began to enter the mainstream of European history through the advent of the Seljuks and draws interesting parallels between the Battle of Hastings in 1066, when the Normans under William the Conqueror invaded England – an event so ingrained into British minds – and the Battle of Manzikert just five years later, in 1071, when the Turks under Sultan Alp Arslan defeated the Roman Byzantines. Both the Normans (descended from Norse Vikings) and the Turks were at first perceived as barbarians, originating from well beyond the areas they came to dominate, 'the one from the fringes of Europe, the other from the fringes of Asia'.[3]

Intermarriage was common between Christians and Muslims, and the Christians of north-west Anatolia continued to practise their faith freely, something that is noted in the letters of the archbishop of Thessalonica in 1354, even as he travelled through the region as an Ottoman prisoner.[4] In fact, there was so much intermarriage between the Ottoman and the Byzantine royal houses that, by the time of the 1453 conquest of Constantinople, one Byzantine scholar commented that Mehmet II had at least as much dynastic claim to the Byzantine throne as many an emperor.[5]

Women played a powerful role from the start, enjoying many more rights in such matters as property ownership, divorce and child custody than their contemporary Western counterparts. Beneath their colourful robes, Turkmen women wore the same baggy şalvar trousers as the men, so that they could fight alongside them astride their horses – never side-saddle – and often with babies strapped to their backs. The trousers, much envied by the first high-society European women to visit Ottoman lands, went on to be adopted by early feminists in England in the 1920s and 1930s, from where they spread to America, renamed 'bloomers' after the women's rights advocate Amelia Jenks Bloomer.

Language wars too are part of the picture, and stereotypes such as 'the terrible Turk'. The West has persisted in labelling the Ottoman Empire as 'Turkey' and its rulers 'Turks'. Yet in Ottoman times the word 'Turk' was used pejoratively to mean 'country bumpkin' or 'illiterate shepherd'. The Ottomans never called themselves 'Turks'. Of the *c.* 250 Ottomans to occupy the role of grand vizier (de facto prime ministers to the sultan), only a minority were ethnically Turkish. The remainder were a mix of Albanian, Circassian, Serbian, Georgian, Greek, Bulgarian, Arab, Armenian, Russian, Hungarian, Chechen, Crimean Tatar and Italian subjects. While the sultan himself was always a Muslim descended from the family of Osman I, founder of the Ottoman dynasty, the top positions were meritocratic, with the talents of all the empire's subjects, of whatever creed or race, deployed to the full. The 'Sick Man of Europe' is another much-used label, but the first to coin it was a Spanish diplomat, describing England in the 1500s. The supposed Ottoman decline, degeneracy and decay that followed the failed second siege of Vienna was a Habsburg myth that cleverly presented 18th-century history as a succession of Habsburg victories against 'the Infidel'. It was achieved through a series of popular Habsburg publications that were widely read throughout Europe.[6]

Only in modern Turkey under Mustafa Kemal Atatürk, after the dissolution of the Ottoman Empire from 1922 onwards, did the word 'Turk' come to be a badge of honour. It remains carved across the hillsides of Anatolia to this day in the Kemalist nationalistic slogan *Ne mutlu Türküm diyene* – 'How happy is he who can call himself a Turk.' The modern Republic of Turkey insisted on the single language, culture and ethnicity of 'Turkishness', expelling the Greeks and banning the Kurdish language, thereby representing the very opposite of the Ottomans' approach, who by no means saw their empire as 'Turkish'.

From the European perspective, the role of Anatolian Turkey across the centuries was to act as a sponge to absorb the chaos of the Middle East and Russia, a view that continues today with the attitude towards Syrian refugees seeking asylum in Europe. The Ottomans introduced a generous 'refugee code' in 1857, yet the Greeks to this day seek to push migrant boats back into Turkish waters, claiming they are 'defending' their borders. The European trope of 'a bridge between East and West' has, like most clichés, some truth in it, but the Ottomans never saw themselves as a bridge or a sponge, and neither do modern Turks for that matter.

In ranging over such a vast subject, encompassing so many dramatic upheavals and metamorphoses in world history, my choices on what to include reflect my own sense of what is important and what is perhaps less well known. Someone else's would, of course, be totally different.

1
The Ottoman Psyche

THE STARTING POINT from which the future Ottoman Empire evolved was a single branch of the powerful Central Asiatic Oghuz tribe. Its early history was oral, only written down years after its rivals had been wiped off the map, but it is the foundation myths as documented by the first Ottoman chroniclers that matter, since they give great insight into the Ottoman psyche. According to their narrative, what distinguished this one tribe of nomadic Turkmens from their neighbours was the dynamic leadership of Ertuğrul, their visionary *bey* (chieftain). Together with his livestock and a relatively small group of loyal Alps – specially trained fighters, skilled in horsemanship, sword-fighting and archery – Ertuğrul migrated westwards across Anatolia to escape the relentless attacks of the Mongols, finally settling on fertile land around Söğüt near Byzantine Nicaea (today's Iznik). This land, where Ertuğrul's son Osman would go on to found the future empire in his name (called *Osmanlı* in Turkish, meaning 'of Osman') in around 1299, was said to have been gifted to them by the Seljuk sultan in return for help defeating their shared Byzantine enemy.

The particular Ottoman identity that gradually emerged in Söğüt was formed from a highly complex mix of cpeting forces within the many surrounding Turkmen *beyliks* (emirates), richly synthesized with Byzantine, Iranian and Armenian elements. The art historian Doğan Kuban has summarized it thus: 'The common feature between Anatolia and all the lands conquered by the Turks in the 12th and 13th centuries was the process of assimilation into their newly conquered lands of all the influences flowing to them from lands they had become connected to by links of culture and political power.'[1]

There is a building that, above all others, captures the essence of this assimilation. It was the very first, along with the world-famous historic sites of Istanbul and the well-documented cave churches of Cappadocia, to be inscribed on Turkey's list of UNESCO World Heritage sites in 1985, when the register was first inaugurated. Yet it is a building few in Europe or the West will have heard of, let alone visited. Rising modestly in a remote valley of central Anatolia, above a small town of the same name, stands the enigmatic mosque–hospital of Divriği, one of the most remarkable and complex structures ever built. It is, quite simply, 'a miracle'.[2] Apart from its highly sophisticated technique of vault construction, one of its many curious components is the way in which the elaborate three-dimensional stone carving on the two entrance portals was consciously contrived to cast the shadow of a giant praying figure. Each is dressed differently – one is thought to be male, the other female – and each changes position inside the portal with the movement of the sun.

Dated 1228–29 and commissioned as a charitable foundation by a man and a woman equally, as individuals – the man the mosque, the woman the hospital – the complex can have been conceived and executed only by the most skilled and flamboyant craftsmen of the time. Yet the Mengücek *beylik* that was responsible for its construction, one of the many Turkish principalities that established themselves in Anatolia, was annihilated just fifty years later by the Mongols under Hulagu. The exuberance of the carving, its sheer energy, was cut short, leaving Divriği an isolated, unfinished building, a brief flowering, for which the politics and the personalities of the time did not align. It is reminiscent of the unfinished Umayyad façade of the Mshatta Palace, now on display in Berlin's Pergamon Museum. After establishing their capital in Damascus in 661, the Umayyads – the first Muslim dynasty – had overseen a similar synthesis. Top craftsmen were brought together in order to create something entirely new, formed from the unique blending of the pre-existing Classical, Byzantine and Sassanian cultures, further enhanced by the fresh approach and energy of the new Muslim rulers. The Syrian Umayyads were snuffed out by the Abbasid caliphs in 750, just a few decades after their architectural style was starting to take shape.

The Umayyad style got a second chance, however, when the dynasty's sole surviving prince escaped across North Africa, bringing the new Islamic elements to Andalusia and refounding Umayyad Syria in Spain. The dynasty went on to rule Andalusia for three centuries and to create the unique culture of Moorish Spain. Explicitly influenced by Islamic architecture, the entrance façade of Antoni Gaudí's basilica of the Sagrada Família cannot but also recall Divriği: that same restless energy and exuberance, that same sense of a giant cosmic tree stretching up to the sky, overflowing with nature's abundance in paradise. Like the project at Divriği, the building is still unfinished, despite Gaudí working on it for thirty-four years until his death. But unlike the Divriği mosque–hospital, which is gently decaying in its forgotten valley, the Sagrada Família is the most visited building in Spain and will be completed, finally, in time for the centenary of the architect's death in 2026.

Here is where the Ottomans were exceptional: they were able to bring their vision to fruition. It is no accident that, in his legendary foundation dream, Osman saw a tree growing from his navel to encompass the world. Like the Mengüceks, Osman's tribe had begun as a small *beylik* living independently under the Seljuks of Konya. Yet, unlike the Mengüceks, their *beylik* survived many setbacks. Over time, they managed to unite with other Turkish *beyliks*, often absorbing the Byzantines along the way through marriages and alliances, until, in 1453, they finally captured the 'Red Apple', as the Byzantine capital, Constantinople, was known. Their early struggles made them tough and adaptable, able to travel and assimilate without surrendering their own sense of who they were. While the word 'Ottoman' conjures up for many Europeans nothing more than a violent military machine propped up by the decadence of Istanbul's harems and hookahs, the real secret of Ottoman success lay in the discipline of their bureaucracy and their army. They harnessed the talents of their diverse populations and introduced a tax regime to encourage enterprise. Their verve and resilience helped them fuse the cultures of Asia, Europe and Africa, absorbing whatever impressed them, from Mongol armour to Persian tilework.

Art historians disagree about many things but concur that it takes centuries for new styles to evolve and find their own form. The Ottomans had 600 years. It was not until the reign of Süleyman (1520–66), called 'the Magnificent' by Western Europeans, and 'the Lawgiver' ('al-Qanuni') by the Ottomans, that their style became fully formed. Displaying itself on the unmistakable Istanbul skyline, pierced with its distinctive array of elegantly contrasting domes and minarets, it was a result of a happy coincidence: the appointment of Sinan, court architect for fifty years, at a time when the empire was at its wealthiest. What the Ottomans bequeathed to the world over the course of their six-century rule, culturally, politically, scientifically and socially, deserves to be fully acknowledged.

Ottoman society from the very beginning was made up of immigrants, uprooted people, agricultural workers in search of pastures, jobless soldiers and landless peasant youths seeking their fortunes and a new life on the Anatolian frontier of the disintegrating Byzantine Empire. 'This was a frontier society in flux,' as the historian Heath Lowry put it. 'As such, it found a place for everyone, free or slave, Muslim or Christian, who had anything to contribute to its growth.'[3] In what had been a highly unstable world, the new Ottoman state brought together different cultures, languages and ethnicities into a centuries-long, stable social and economic system sometimes styled the 'Pax Ottomana'. Provided they paid their taxes and remained loyal, subjects of any ethnicity or religion could live free from coercion and manage their own internal affairs under the protection of the Ottoman state.

It was a core principle throughout Ottoman rule that everyone, including refugees, should be welcomed – a principle that first manifested itself after the Reconquista, when tens of thousands of Jews expelled from Spain by the Catholic monarchs Ferdinand and Isabella in 1492 were invited to found prosperous communities in towns under the protection of the Ottoman sultans. Later, in the 16th century, many groups of Moriscos (former Muslims forced to convert to Christianity by the Catholic Church in Spain) expelled from Andalusia were settled in the Galata district of Istanbul. In the last centuries of the empire, the Ottoman state welcomed and settled hundreds of thousands of refugees fleeing from the Russian invasions of the Balkans, Circassia and Crimea. The policy continued under the modern republic, when Turkey took in the Kirghiz of Afghanistan escaping the Soviet occupation in the 1980s, then provided refuge and support for millions of Syrians fleeing the ongoing war in their homeland. A wave of refugees from the collapsing Afghan state in 2021 is but the latest to arrive.

Alongside their essential rigour and steel, the Ottomans saw no contradiction in enjoying the finer aspects of life, unafraid, even as rugged fighters, to display their love of gardens and flowers, especially the tulip and the rose. This unusual weave of Turkish identity can be seen most strongly in boldly colourful tents and textiles, things to be worn or folded and carried on the back of a horse. Behind the fine robes, carpets and ceramics on display in their headquarters, Istanbul's Topkapı Palace, lie centuries of migration, trade and struggle.

'The Eternal State' (Turkish *Devlet-i Ebed-muddet*) was the official Ottoman motto. Osman always had aspirations to found a state, as is clear from the fact that he minted coins in the name of 'Osman son of Ertuğrul' – from which we also know that Ertuğrul was not just a fabrication of early chronicles. Born in Söğüt in around 1258 as the third son of Ertuğrul, he died in nearby Bursa, the first Ottoman capital, in 1326. Both he and his father before him were accompanied by a variety of wandering dervishes (Muslim holy men, often mystics) who helped provide spiritual guidance and whose loyal presence at the very earliest times in the formation of the empire led to a close and long-standing relationship between early dervish orders and the Ottoman state. Granted land to found their lodges, known as *tekkes*, these orders, such as the Bektashis, helped popularize Islam, making it accessible to local people and attracting settlement into newly conquered areas.[4]

The Byzantine Empire was known to be in its final throes, severely weakened by the Fourth Crusade in 1204, when the Norman Crusaders, aided by the Venetians, had attacked their co-religionists the Greek Orthodox in their capital Constantinople, stripping the city of its riches. The Byzantine elite that survived became increasingly impoverished, and in their desperation they imposed oppressive taxes on their destitute subjects, treating them cruelly. The Latin Templar Crusaders were also involved, seeking to undermine both the last remnants of the Byzantine state and the Seljuk sultanate based at Konya. In this environment of competing forces Ertuğrul and his Alps, given their small numbers, were not at first seen as a threat and were underestimated. Derided by his enemies as a barbarian Turk, a mere shepherd with no education or sophistication, Ertuğrul acknowledged that his tribe, as a nomad group, did indeed lack trading experience, honest merchants, craftsmen, skilled artisans and poets. He recognized that he would need such people to help build up a prosperous state that was free from corruption and where the poor would be looked after. This was another reason why newcomers and strangers (*gharib*, from the Arabic for 'outsider') with skills were welcomed, be they disillusioned Byzantines, Armenians or any other group looking to settle. He is said to have proclaimed to his followers: 'Give the work to its expert. If we become an ocean, all rivers will flow to us. There will be justice and order in the lands and our state will show mercy.'

Many joined Ertuğrul as his reputation grew. His was also the only Islamic *beylik* to share a frontier with the poorly defended Byzantine territory to the west – another factor that drew Turkmens escaping the long Mongol reach and likewise looking for new opportunities to live in safety in new and prosperous lands. His choice of Söğüt as the place to settle was a highly conscious and considered decision. Though today the town seems like an insignificant backwater, in the mid-1200s it occupied a strategical position at the centre of a network of important trade routes. Situated on a well-defended hill, it dominated the main road between Konya and Constantinople. The surrounding landscape offered rich grazing land, fertile soil, olive trees and vineyards. Ertuğrul's tomb today stands proudly in Söğüt, where there is also an ethnographic museum showcasing the social customs and dress of the period.

Osman continued his father's approach and methods as he further expanded the beylik, pushing back the Byzantine border at its weakest point to the west. With each Byzantine town that fell, more and more soldiers from the Byzantine army defected to the Ottoman side. Over time, many converted to Islam, not under Ottoman pressure but out of a natural desire to assume the identity of the winning side. When negotiations following the siege of Bursa were ongoing, for example, the Byzantine minister there decided to join the Ottomans rather than return to Constantinople, telling Orhan, Osman's son and successor as sultan: 'Your state is growing bigger and bigger every day. Ours has turned.' The other Turkish Anatolian *beyliks* that had surrounded Orhan to the north, the south and the east all slipped one by one under the suzerainty of the advancing Mongols. The Black Death, which raged from around 1346 to 1353, was another factor at this time, weakening the sedentary Byzantine urban populations and favouring nomadic tent-living whereby space and fresh air were easy to come by.

During their first two centuries the Ottomans expanded mainly into Europe, the Byzantine Empire's weakest and most vulnerable point. Macedonia, Serbia and Bulgaria all fell in quick succession before the end of the 14th century, and the Ottomans continued their approach of religious tolerance and integration of existing traditions well into the 1500s.

Forced migrations did, however, take place: the Ottomans moved people from the newly conquered Balkan countries to Constantinople to repopulate it and revitalize its economy, much diminished during the Byzantines' twilight days. The Balkan countries were also the preferred source of talent to be drafted into the *devşirme* system, in which young boys, usually between 8 and 15 years of age, were taken from towns and villages every four or five years to form a reservoir of future soldiers free from family and tribal loyalties. Once separated from their families, they were taken to Istanbul, circumcised, converted to Islam and given a formal education. While there are accounts of desperate mothers trailing after the Ottoman soldiers lamenting the loss of their sons, there are also stories of families, especially Albanians and Bosnians, volunteering their male offspring, seeing it as an opportunity for their child to rise to the very top of the Ottoman system – which the most talented did. All of the grand viziers between 1400 and 1600 advanced in this way, including Sinan the court architect, Rüstem Pasha, who married the sultan's daughter, and Sokullu Pasha, grand vizier to Süleyman the Magnificent. The system also produced most of the empire's military commanders and provincial governors.

The *devşirme* system effectively ended *c.* 1648, but it is worth explaining its origins, as it goes right to the heart of early Ottoman meritocratic thinking, whereby work was given to the person most able to perform it well – 'the best person for the job', irrespective of their class, family, religion or ethnicity. The system was consistent with the Ottomans' approach of maximizing everyone's talents for the good of the state. It may also have been a way of thinking influenced by an older Turkish tradition, in which highly trained Turkish slave units – 'Mamluks', from the Arabic word meaning 'owned' – were used in Arab armies. The term did not share the exact connotations of 'slave', however, since the Mamluks were not an underclass: they were schooled to become a military and social elite. Mamluk dynasties even went on to rule India, Egypt and Syria. The system followed strict rules: advance notice had to be given of their arrival in every town, sons of widows could not be taken, and neither could only sons. Those showing special talent and promise would be chosen, be they Christian, Jewish, Greek, Slav, Armenian, Berber, Arab, black or white. Complications of tribal loyalties were thereby avoided, creating a military and a civil service that owed its allegiance solely to the Ottoman state. As such, it was the first professional system of government in the region, entirely meritocratic rather than aristocratic, the norm of the time.[5] It took many centuries before European countries achieved anything of equal efficiency.

The Ottoman Empire was perhaps the most cosmopolitan state in the world, with approximately 30 million subjects at its peak. Ethnically and linguistically diverse, encompassing over seventy and one-half ethnic groupings (the Roma were recognized as the half – more than any European nation has ever granted them), it also had at least twelve different languages. Bilingualism and trilingualism were commonplace, particularly in urban centres, and in no province of the empire was there a unique language. At the peak of Ottoman power,

Persian and Arabic vocabulary still accounted for up to 88 per cent of Ottoman Turkish, and words of Arabic origin heavily outnumbered native Turkish words. Today few Arabs from the former Ottoman provinces speak Turkish, and in the Balkans most speak only the national tongue of their own country, with the result that many communities can no longer easily communicate with each other and are in danger of becoming increasingly isolationist.

Mehmet II – named 'the Conqueror' after taking Istanbul in 1453 and ending Byzantine rule, although he was a young man of only 21 at the time – was well versed in Greek and Christian culture, with Greek and Latin classics in his personal library. He regarded Hagia Sophia as an outstanding achievement and, on converting it to a mosque, did not make any significant alterations to the structure, only to the decor. In discussion with experts, he helped plan the curriculum of Ottoman schools. As well as courses in Islamic jurisprudence, geometry, geography, astronomy and medicine, he included a course in the 'art of speaking and expressing yourself well and kindly' (see plate 6).

Ottoman Turkish gradually replaced Arabic and Persian as the language of scholarship, and Turkish itself also changed, moving away from Central Asian Turkic and closer to Persian dialects, in a process similar to the way in which Latin ceased to be the lingua franca of European scholarship in favour of local spoken languages. Turkish belongs to the group of languages known as Ural–Altaic, utterly different from the familiar Indo-European structure of Persian/Farsi and the Semitic Arabic. Yet the early Ottomans and their Seljuk ancestors displayed an astonishing ability to absorb all three – Turkish, Persian and Arabic – with remarkable fluency, even writing in more than one of them. The advantage of trilingualism is not merely being able to communicate across cultures. Its benefits are now also known to extend to better memory, better multi-tasking, better critical thinking and better problem-solving – in other words, much higher cognitive skills, more creativity and greater mental flexibility across the board.

Sometimes words are shared across all three languages, one interesting example being *Amen*, used by Christians at the end of prayers as a confirmatory response. Originally appearing in the Hebrew Bible, it is also found in the Greek New Testament. Islam uses it in exactly the same way in Arabic, Persian and Turkish. Its literal meaning in all three is 'We are believers', often said with the palm of the hand held to the heart to reinforce affirmation.

After Sultan Selim Yavuz ('Yavuz' is translated as 'the Grim' by Europeans and 'the Resolute' by Turks) conquered the Arab lands of Syria and Palestine from the Byzantines in 1516, the new Ottoman regime took very seriously its duty of care over the holy sites and its role as guardian of the route for pilgrims on the Hajj to Mecca, realizing that they were the first non-Arab Muslims to enjoy that prestige. The Ottomans now appeared to abandon much of the pragmatism of their early centuries when their empire had been majority Christian. From 1517 onwards, now that most subjects were Muslim, they presented them-selves as defenders of the Sunni orthodoxy against the Persian Shi'a Safavids.

To demonstrate their Islamic credentials in Jerusalem, the Ottoman authorities quickly set about restoring the dilapidated Dome of the Rock. The site has ancient, pre-Islamic origins, housing the sacred stone where Abraham is said to have been asked by God to sacrifice Isaac; it is also holy to Muslims as the place where the Prophet Muhammad is said to have begun his nocturnal journey to heaven on his steed, Buraq. The Ottomans employed craftsmen from Tabriz to make tiles for the exterior, since the tradition of covering the exterior of holy buildings with tiles was common in Persia, though unknown in other Islamic countries at the time. The techniques used were Persian as well – the *cuerda seca* method, for instance, which stops colours running during firing – and a tile inscription over the north portico door dated 1552 bears the name 'Abdullah of Tabriz'. After the defeat of the Safavid Persians at Çaldıran in 1514, local craftsmen were captured and also put to work in Istanbul.

Damascus had surrendered to Sultan Selim without a fight, but it was not till 1554, under Süleyman the Magnificent, that the Ottomans put their mark on the city, constructing their first mosque there: the Tekkiye Süleymaniye, a Sufi dervish centre unlike anything else in the city. The Ottoman attitude – unlike that of their Mamluk predecessors, who endowed mosques and madrasas as close to the city centres of Cairo and Damascus as possible – was not to interfere with the existing mosques, but rather to build on the edges of cities, so as to avoid the destruction of earlier sites. The Tekkiye, designed by Sinan but built by local craftsmen, was deliberately sited on the outskirts near the Barada River, on open ground used by pilgrims on their way to Mecca. It was part of a complex of buildings, typical to Ottoman culture but previously unknown in Syria, designed not only to be a place of worship but also to provide accommodation for pilgrims, shops, kitchens and a madrasa (Turkish *medrese*) for religious study – a uniquely Ottoman blend of buildings serving social, religious and commercial purposes. It was a powerful statement of the new Ottoman dominion, yet at a respectful distance from the Great Umayyad Mosque at the heart of the old walled city. The Ottomans made interesting concessions to the local style, such as the decision to employ *ablaq* masonry, with its alternating stripes of black basalt and white limestone, demonstrating a sensitivity to local tastes and traditions. For all that, the Tekkiye Mosque itself, completed in 1556, is unmistakably Ottoman in style, with its twin pencil minarets, cube structure surmounted by a single hemispherical dome and multi-domed portico.

This Ottoman approach to integrating its new Muslim subjects in the Arab world was the same as that already adopted in the 14th century in the Balkan Christian–Byzantine countries, and when the empire absorbed refugees, including the Jews exiled from Spain in the late 15th century. By founding public structures such as mosques, markets, hammams (better known as 'Turkish baths') and fountains throughout the cities they conquered, the Ottomans asserted their patronage and authority while integrating their presence alongside existing structures. The oldest surviving Ottoman structure in Europe is a public kitchen established by Gazi Evrenos Bey in Komotini, present-day north-eastern Greece, which served both to feed the poor and to provide dervish accommodation. As adherents of the Hanafi school of Islamic law, for whom ablutions before prayer must be performed under running water (*hanafia* today still means 'tap' in colloquial Arabic), the Ottomans are especially associated with water systems, fountains and hammams. Responsibility for the system that fed all the capital's imperial buildings fell to Sinan, court architect from 1538, and before embarking on the construction of any new mosque he would first ensure its water supply. So important was this role that Inspector of Waterworks (*Suyolu Nazırı*) became a separate post in 1566; entrusted with construction, maintenance and repair, the office-holder was responsible for the water supply not just in Istanbul, but in all the provincial cities of the empire.

Even Turk-hating Budapest, today the capital of Hungary, has four Turkish baths from the Ottoman era still functioning and open to the public. Most Balkan towns were endowed with a Turkish bath, though many are gently falling into ruin or, in a handful of cases, have been converted into public spaces such as exhibition halls. Ottoman fountains can still be seen in city centres and town squares throughout the former empire. Even in Vienna, an Ottoman-style fountain stands in the Türkenschanzpark (named after the entrenchments dug by the Ottomans during the first siege of Vienna in 1529) commemorating Yunus Emre, a famous Sufi mystic poet who greatly influenced Turkish culture; it was a gift from the Turkish ambassador as a token of Austro-Turkish friendship, unveiled in 1991.

While the Divriği miracle stands as a medieval herald to the Ottomans, there is also a little-known 21st-century painting that likewise illustrates the complications associated with assessing the Ottomans and their legacy. A pair of botanical drawings on display in the British Museum's 2021 exhibition 'Reflections: Contemporary Art of the Middle East and North Africa', by the artist Aslı Çavuşoğlu, a Turk born in Istanbul in 1982, is painted in shades of red ink derived from the Armenian cochineal beetle. The beetle has its habitat on the banks of the Aras River, which forms the border between Turkey and Armenia, but today it is an endangered species. Traditionally, it was used by skilled Armenian craftsmen to make a red dye for textiles. The fainter shades of red

represent both the beetle's loss through environmental deg-
radation in present-day Armenia and the loss of Armenian
lives during the genocide and expulsions of 1915, while the
stronger hue represents the Turkish flag.

2
The Commercial Spirit

SOCIAL DIVERSITY WAS always at the core of the Ottoman way of thinking, and commercial matters were no exception. From the outset there was an awareness that trade could flourish only if it were open to all, facilitated wherever possible by various institutions of the state. The most obvious example was the caravanserai network, which the Ottomans inherited in Anatolia from the Seljuks and later expanded into the Balkans, whereby the state provided a safe environment to encourage free movement and commerce. Accommodation was gratis for all merchants of whatever religion or ethnicity.

The aim of the early Ottomans was to institute a new system, based first and foremost round the needs of the community. They had witnessed the final decay of the Byzantine administration in the lands they conquered around Karacahisar, Bilecik and Söğüt, and saw how the various Christian governors lived in castles remote from their subjects, raking in vast sums through exploitation of the poor and hefty taxes. Market places were run by greedy merchants who were allied to them.

The *külliye* system, which would become a key institution, characterized the Ottoman approach, offering a blend of social, commercial, religious, educational and charitable functions. The original *külliye* complex was built in Bursa, the first

Ottoman capital. A clue to its purpose and scope can be found in the name, which is derived from the Arabic *kull*, meaning 'all' – in other words, it was an inclusive complex for everyone, not just the elite. (It is worth stressing here that the English word *college* is completely unrelated to the *külliye* concept – on the contrary, it is derived from the Latin verb *lego*, meaning 'to select', and the preposition *cum*. A college is thus only for those who have been selected to attend, just as our English word *colleagues* means 'people who have been selected to work together'.)

The model for the *külliye* was familiar to the Ottomans through similar institutions set up by their Seljuk predecessors, and also drew on the pre-existing Byzantine tradition whereby many of the great Byzantine monasteries, especially in Constantinople, incorporated places of learning and charitable institutions.[1] But, as was frequently the case, the Ottomans amalgamated the best of both practices and developed them further.

The distinctive feature of the *külliye* system was that the money from the profit-earning components – chiefly the market and the hammam (public baths) – was directed back into the complex. This money then funded the maintenance of the mosque at the heart of the *külliye*, the salary of the imam and the *muezzin*, and the upkeep of the school (*medrese*), the dervish hostel (*tekke* or *zaviye*), hospital/clinic (*dur al-shifa*), old people's home (*dar al-ajouz*), the bakery and the soup kitchen (*imaret*) for the poor. No one individual could make a personal profit from such a set-up, since it was endowed as a charitable religious trust, called a *waqf* (Turkish *vakıf*), in perpetuity.

As the needs of the community grew and became more complex over the centuries, so too the *külliye* system expanded to fulfil these needs. The buildings acquired more annexes to provide for further education, for instance, including medical schools and law schools. The peak of such development is represented by the Süleymaniye, designed on an Istanbul hilltop by the court architect Sinan for Süleyman the Magnificent in 1550: it has a total of seven schools attached, making it both the scientific and the cultural centre of Istanbul and the empire. Just over half of the 3,523 craftsmen who worked on it were Christian.[2]

Bursa, captured from the Byzantines after a lengthy siege in 1328, had been a major trading hub based on the local manufacture of silk cloth, woven from raw silk imported from Iran. In preindustrial and early industrial societies, textiles frequently played a key role in trade: fabrics held the same position as iron and steel did from the mid-19th century onwards, the chemical industries from the 1890s, electrical equipment from the 1930s to the 1970s, and computer industries from then to the present.

UNESCO put Bursa on its World Heritage List in 2014, along with surrounding villages such as Cumalıkızık, because together they illustrate the exceptional urban planning that accompanied the birth of the Ottoman Empire in the 14th and early 15th centuries. The first five Ottoman sultans conceived them as an integrated whole, embodying the key functions of the social and economic organization of Bursa around a civic centre. It was a deliberate Ottoman approach: society was supported by careful urban planning, with Osman founding seven *waqf* villages in the hillsides around Bursa, one for each of his sons and their wives, in perpetuity. A few of these villages still survive, of which Cumalıkızık is the best preserved; its function was explicitly to provide income for the *külliye* of Osman's son, Orhan. Residential housing gradually built up round the *külliyes*, which themselves remain in use, their original functions adapted to 21st-century life. In the Muradiye complex in Bursa, for instance, completed in 1426, the Ottoman public kitchen is used today as a restaurant, and the hammam is a centre for physically challenged people. In the Green Mosque complex, the madrasa is now the Museum of Turkish Islamic Art.

Bursa was therefore created and managed by the first Ottoman sultans through an innovative and ingenious system developed around what UNESCO calls 'an unprecedented urban planning process'. As the first capital of the empire, it served as the model Ottoman city, later referenced throughout the expanding Ottoman Empire. The UNESCO entry continues: 'The new capital, with its social, religious and commercial functions, reflects the values of the society and the values it accepted from its neighbours, during long years of migration from central Asia to the West. This is also reflected in the integration of Byzantine, Seljuk, Arab, Persian and other influences in architectural stylistics ... Many sultans and courtiers, then the leaders of the Muslim World, recognized the importance of Bursa as the spiritual capital of the Ottoman Empire, even after the conquest of Istanbul, and demonstrated their loyalty to their ancestors and the city, by choosing Bursa as the location for burial.'[3] In addition to the early tombs of Osman and Orhan, Bursa also boasts the Muradiye complex, named after Murad II, which houses many later tombs.

The market area, with its collection of khans (Turkish *hans*, meaning 'caravanserais') built round a courtyard, still serves as the commercial hub of the city. The UNESCO entry recognizes the special atmosphere of these Ottoman trading centres, where traditional rituals such as bargaining continue in a timeless manner.

Thanks to meticulous Ottoman record-keeping, we know that in the year 1487 there were 6,457 tax-paying heads of households in Bursa, from which scholars and researchers have been able to estimate that the city's population numbered about 40,000, a little less than half that of Istanbul at the time.[4] Ottoman archives also show that all mosques and schools founded by the sultan were funded by the *waqf* system, according to which surrounding shops, khans and weighing scales (*kapan*) provided extensive sources of income for the foundation. Thus the Great Mosque (Ulu Cami) of Bursa, begun in 1396 and completed in 1400, was surrounded by several khans and a covered market. Bursa's Ulu Cami foundation boasted sixty-seven shops.[5] The nearby mosque of Osman's son – the second Ottoman ruler, Orhan Gazi (r. 1326–52) – derived much of its income from land but also had 214 shops and urban real estate on which tanneries were built. Murad I (r. 1352–89), the third Ottoman ruler, donated several villages to his pious foundation but also had ample urban revenues from shops and even a workshop manufacturing millet beer (*bozahane*).[6]

Merchants from Florence are recorded as appearing in Bursa in the 15th century, as are Shi'ite merchants bringing in raw silk from Shirvan in today's Azerbaijan. Local *qadi* (judge) registers survive from the 1480s till the end of the Ottoman Empire, providing a window onto the city's social and economic life, and the court cases reveal all manner of disputes associated with local silk manufacture. Nearby Iznik, then known as Nicaea, had also once served as a silk-weaving city in the 13th century, in the twilight days of the Byzantine Empire, so it is possible that some surviving weavers transferred to serve the Bursa court of

Orhan Gazi around 1326. In the 15th and 16th centuries caravans from Iran carried the raw silk to Bursa, arriving via Erzurum or Diyarbakır, or via Tokat and Amasya. This movement was disrupted by the Safavid wars between Sultan Selim I and Shah Ismail, founder of the Safavid dynasty, during which Iranian merchants foolish enough to enter Ottoman territories could find themselves kidnapped and their wares confiscated. As a result, the import of raw silk into Ottoman territory was taken up largely by Armenians from Iran, who could not be suspected of being religious leaders of the Safavid order in disguise – 'an idée fixe of Ottoman mid-16th century Ottoman administrators whenever Muslim travellers from Iran were concerned'.[7]

In the 16th century records show that liturgical vestments manufactured in Bursa were used in Orthodox church services. Other non-royal customers were wealthy Polish noblemen, who in the 17th century adopted the so-called 'Sarmathian' style of silk clothing strongly inspired by Ottoman models, supposedly worn by their legendary ancestors. Some of these exotic garments served as grave clothes, while others were used as vestments by Catholic priests. Maria Theresa wears a dress of Ottoman silk in a painting by the Swedish-Austrian court painter Martin van Meytens dated 1743/44, which depicts the empress in 'Turkish costume'.[8]

Silk was not the only textile worked by Bursa artisans: cotton, both on its own and combined with silk, had also become popular as a cheaper alternative. The mix was known as *kutnı* (from the Arabic *qutun*, the origin of our English word 'cotton') and was dyed in dark colours to serve as skirts for non-Muslim women.[9] From 1600 onwards Bursa served not only the Ottoman court but also the residents of Istanbul, the Anatolian market and foreign customers, especially in Eastern Europe.

When wars disrupted the Iranian supply chain and Bursa began cultivating its own raw silk in the 1600s, it exported not only finished silks to centres such as the capital, but also raw silks to emergent markets like Chios in the mid-18th century.[10]

As the Industrial Revolution gathered pace in the 1830s, the silk industrialists of Lyon and the United Kingdom 'discovered' the mulberry groves around Bursa as a source of raw material. They encouraged the establishment of factories, in which a largely female workforce reeled and twisted silk thread adapted to the weaving of damasks, jacquards and other fancy fabrics that mechanized looms could now produce.[11]

Women in the workforce and as powerful benefactors

It was customary in Ottoman cities for workers to come together in craft guilds that could protect the interests of the guild masters, for example by limiting the numbers of work-shops that could operate in the city. Bursa women, although they rarely owned silk-weaving looms, formed an important part of the workforce. Some were weavers, while others reeled or twisted silk thread. In 17th-century Istanbul, Ottoman archives show that there were women silk embroiderers with workshops of their own, and we know that some women in Bursa manu-factured silk braid for decorating garments and possessed the right to market their products wherever they pleased, without paying any dues, much to the chagrin of the male Bursa silk merchants. In 1678 women in Bursa owned about one-half of the silk-reeling and -twisting equipment (*mancınık*), so were evi-dently independent agents, albeit of modest means, rather than mere appendages to their husbands' enterprises.[12]

Ottoman women controlled a great deal of wealth in their own right, independent of their spouses. They had the freedom to invest in businesses or establish mosques and madrasas, part of a long tradition of women endowing such institutions that had begun under the Seljuks and continued under the Ottomans. Of the six mosque complexes built in Istanbul by Süleyman the Magnificent's family, for instance, three were commissioned by women. His mother, Hafsa Sultan, built a complex in Manisa consisting of a mosque, madrasa, hospice, primary school, kitchen, hospital and bathhouse employing 100 people. Mihrimah (see plate 3), Süleyman's daughter, the richest woman in the world at that time, built similar complexes in Istanbul, one at Üsküdar (see plate 4) and the other at the Edirne Gate, both designed by Sinan. Süleyman's wife, Hürrem Haseki (Roxelana), endowed large mosque complexes in Istanbul, Edirne, Jerusalem, Mecca and Medina. That at Jerusalem included a 55-room hospice, a bakery, an inn and a stable. The Yeni Valide Mosque on the Golden Horn was begun by the mother of one sultan (Murad IV) and completed by the mother of another (Turhan); and the maintenance of the mosque, madrasa, library, fountain and tomb was ensured in perpetuity by the income from the nearby Mısır Çarşısı (Egyptian Bazaar) and a caravanserai. Voltaire commented on the contrast between the freedom of Ottoman women and that of women in France, writing in 1765 that women in Islam 'are by no means slaves; they have property; they can make wills, they are able to request a divorce on occasion.'

In Aleppo in the mid-1700s, women constituted up to one-third of all commercial property buyers and investors; and because the property laws in the Ottoman Empire were more favourable to women than in Western Europe, Christian women wanting to secure a fairer deal often preferred the Muslim courts over their own Orthodox ones, which were usually run by the clergy. The rights of women were grounded in traditional Islam, and of course the Prophet Muhammad's first wife, Khadija, was herself a merchant, wealthy in her own right and running her own business. She was twice widowed, with six children from her first two husbands; Muhammad, her junior by fifteen years, began his working life as her employee, leading her trade caravans to Syria. He did not take another wife till after her death, sixteen years later.

Transport

Constant comings and goings were the norm in the trading cities of the Ottoman Empire, despite the later sultans' frequent admonishments of their subjects, who were urged to stay in one place and pay their taxes. Western historians of the 19th and 20th centuries frequently claimed that edicts of this sort led to stagnation in Ottoman commerce, but the researches of scholars such as Suraiya Faroqhi into the Ottoman archives and court records show that, in Bursa at any rate, the opposite was often true.[13]

A huge amount of movement took place within the empire, not least the enormous migrations and deportations of the late 1800s and early 1900s. Ottoman officialdom was keen to settle nomads and establish security on the roads, in the interests of maximizing trade through the free movement of merchants between markets. They took the view that commerce would thrive and the tax revenues to the treasury would rise, thereby ensuring a prosperous people and state. Modern Turkey under President Erdoğan has broadly followed a similar policy in recent decades – some might even call it 'neo-Ottoman' – spending millions on high-speed rail infrastructure and regional airports. This certainly brought prosperity in the

1990s and 2000s to far-flung areas of central and eastern Turkey through greater connectivity, but new schemes for canals and ever-bigger bridges to cross the Bosphorus are widely seen more as vanity projects than true expansions.

The Ottomans too concerned themselves not just with land links between cities, but also with bridges, river transportation, ferryboats and even the upkeep of urban pavements. They laid the groundwork for much of the transport network that is still used today across their former empire, in the Balkans, in Turkey itself, and in Syria and Egypt. The purpose of the Hejaz railway, whose completion was interrupted by the First World War, was not just to link Istanbul to Mecca for the annual pilgrimage, but also to improve the economic integration of distant Arabian provinces into the Ottoman state. It was begun in Damascus in 1900, and by 1908 it had reached Medina in the Hejaz, making the Hajj to Mecca far more accessible and faster than the slow and dangerous camel caravans of the past. The railway was built to a very high standard at very low cost, in one of the fastest such projects ever completed anywhere in the world.[14]

The Hajj to Mecca was another reason to travel – one whose commercial opportunities the Ottomans were also keen to maximize, especially after their conquest of the Arab lands of Syria and Egypt, through which the pilgrim caravans had to travel. The Hajj itself has often been likened to a great river of commerce, as indeed were all pilgrim routes, such as those to the Holy Land and to European shrines including Santiago de Compostela. Poorer pilgrims would take items from their home provinces to sell along the way or on arrival to help offset travel expenses, and they would buy items to sell on their return. The Ottoman traveller Evliya Çelebi, who spent forty years on the road in the middle of the 17th century moving round the empire at its cultural zenith, gives detailed accounts of the buying and selling that went on in Mecca during the pilgrimage season, with the sheriffs of Mecca holding fairs to facilitate trade among wealthier merchants from all across the empire.[15]

In the 16th and early 17th centuries, hundreds of Ottoman merchants – Jews, Muslims and Christians – travelled widely, especially to Venice. In crossing the Adriatic from one of the sultan's ports, they would quite often fall prey to pirates, particularly the so-called Uskoks, border warriors loosely controlled by the Habsburgs, who did not hesitate to attack Christian merchants for 'doing business with the infidel'.[16] In the 18th century Orthodox merchants from the Balkans also undertook much long-distance trade, often marketing the goods that family members and fellow villagers had produced during the winter. The fairs of Leipzig were a common destination, for example. Merchants were obliged to pay tolls on entering the Habsburg or Ottoman domains, depending on their direction of travel.[17]

It was not just merchants who undertook long journeys. Craftsmen and labourers travelled too, in search of more lucrative work. If agricultural workers wanted to leave, however, they had first to obtain permission from the person who collected their taxes and administered their village.[18] This was because land was only profitable if there were enough people to work it, and sometimes court records show that peasants were obliged by landowners to return unless they had been absent for over ten years, after which they were considered lost forever. The collection of taxes was a priority for the Ottomans throughout the centuries, and former nomads were encouraged to settle down in towns or villages – either voluntarily, for economic reasons, or under state pressure and against their will, so that they became tax-paying citizens.

England became an Ottoman ally from the 1570s after the pope excommunicated the Protestant Queen Elizabeth I. From that point on, the two states shared a common enemy in the Catholic Habsburgs based in Vienna and Spain. In 1578 the English queen initiated a correspondence with the Ottoman sultan about trade privileges, seeking new trade relations beyond Europe. Elizabeth was asking for nothing less than free access to the markets of the Islamic world through the gateway of Constantinople in order to bypass her enemy, the Catholic Philip II of Spain. She wrote:

> Most Imperial and Most Invincible Emperor,
> We have received the letters of your Mighty Highness written
> to us from Constantinople whereby we understand how
> graciously and how favourably the humble petition of one
> William Harebroom was granted to him and his company.
> We desire of Your Highness that the commendation of such
> singular courtesy may be enlarged to all our subjects in general.

As part of the diplomatic wooing process, Elizabeth sent the sultan exotic English gifts, including a clockwork organ and Thomas Dallam – 'Honest Tom', its Lancastrian manufacturer – to turn the handle, much to the delight and fascination of Murad III.[19] In return, he and the sultana sent back perfumes, soaps and silks. Mutually beneficial trading links were then established, according to which England exported to the Ottoman Empire tin and lead, stripped from Catholic churches and monasteries. The Ottomans recycled these metals into the weaponry they then used against Catholic Spain – an irony that would have been appreciated by both Elizabeth and the English court.

The Provinces

Of course, it is Istanbul, Ottoman capital for nearly 500 years, that boasts the biggest business district in the former empire – a place where sultans, their mothers, their viziers and less well-known investors constructed many business-related structures, including caravanserais. There was also the ancient Kapalıçarşı district (today's famous Grand Bazaar, where more than 4,000 shops are spread over 61 covered streets), which grew up around the two covered markets originally established by Mehmet the Conqueror, who reigned for thirty years till 1481.

But much commercial activity also took place in the provinces. In Syria, Süleyman the Magnificent appointed his confidant and hunting companion Şemsi Ahmet Pasha to be the Ottoman governor-general of Damascus in the 1550s. Once there, Şemsi spotted a commercial opportunity and became the first to import the newly discovered commodity of Yorkshire broadcloth, highly valued for its hardwearing quality and warmth. Alongside conducting his official business of supervising the construction of Süleyman's Tekkiye Mosque on the outskirts of the city, he ordered the first stone-domed structure to be built in the heart of the old city to store his precious cloth. Called the Khan al-Joukhiyya (*joukh* is Arabic for 'broadcloth'), it is today the oldest surviving Ottoman khan in Damascus, and is still in use. Şemsi's entrepreneurial spirit lives on in his 21st-century Syrian descendants, the Chamsi-Pasha family, who continue to sell broadcloth all round the world from their Yorkshire headquarters. The German architectural historian Stefan Weber, now director of Berlin's Islamic Art Museum, describes how such stone-domed khans in Ottoman Damascus had become 'veritable cathedrals of commerce' by the 18th century.[20] In Damascus alone, the many centuries of Ottoman rule left a legacy of 57 commercial complexes, 18 of which are still functioning in the old city. Even so, it is a mere fraction of Cairo's 145, and substantially below Aleppo's 77, many of which also still survive, in spite of the Syrian civil war.

It was, however, the Balkans that formed the real power base and contained the richest and most populous provinces of the empire.[21] Sadly, most of the khans and souks established there during the centuries of Ottoman rule have been destroyed or allowed to fall into ruin since the anti-Ottoman backlash that accompanied the rise of nationalism in the 19th century. The bazaars at Skopje, today the capital of North Macedonia, and at Novi Pazar (New Market) in Serbia form two notable exceptions.

Khan As'ad Pasha al-'Azem

For all their past wealth, however, the Balkans can boast nothing on the scale of the magnificent nine-domed Khan As'ad Pasha in Damascus, the apogee of all commercial buildings in the city (see plate 5). Trade in Damascus flourished especially in the 18th and 19th centuries, and the khans gradually increased in size as a consequence. Built by a wealthy member of the 'Azem family, many of whom rose to be the city's governors, its massive stone-carved entrance portal in the heart of the souks, completed in 1753, is the city's grandest. The design of the khan, with its nine small domes and central huge dome, is reminiscent of the Persian style of khan, and the nine domes are part of the Shi'a tradition. The blended architectural styles again reflect the fact that the priority of the Ottoman authorities was to raise taxes from the provinces, not to impose a Turkish identity on them. Every notable businessman in Damascus would have rented a room here. The covered courtyard, with its colossal ceiling height, gave protection from the extremes of weather in winter and summer. The inside space has been likened to St Peter's Basilica in Rome. Before the onset of civil war in Syria, it was in use as an exhibition space, and in 2008 even hosted a ceramics exhibition organized by London's Victoria and Albert Museum.[22]

When Ottoman power began to decline, the imperial system established in the Arab provinces simply concentrated on the essentials, namely providing protection for pilgrims on the Hajj. This is what gave the Ottoman state its legitimacy, and the organization of the pilgrimage began to dominate all aspects of Syria's activities. Damascus could not be allowed to slip into decay and anarchy because it played a vital role as an assembly point for all pilgrims from the north and east, while those from the west congregated at Cairo.

Trade deals, demise and legacy

In 1838 the United Kingdom and the Ottoman Empire signed the Anglo-Ottoman Treaty, a formal trade deal that imposed some of the most liberal open-market settlements ever seen, whereby the Ottomans would abolish all monopolies and allow British merchants full access to all Ottoman markets, taxed at the same rate as local merchants. Meanwhile, the United Kingdom continued to employ protectionist policies within its own agricultural markets. The resulting rapid influx of cheap British textiles crippled the Ottoman textile manufacturing business, making it near impossible for the Ottoman Empire to industrialize. An 1866 Ottoman report cited that the number of textile looms in Istanbul and Üsküdar had fallen from 2,730 to just 23. The number of brocade looms fell from 350 to only 4, while in Aleppo cotton looms fell from 40,000 to only 5,000.

This integration into the European-dominated world market continued till 1914, when the export market collapsed completely owing to the First World War.

And yet the Ottoman superpower had played a substantial part in shaping the business practices of modern Europe. Venice and its powerful Habsburg allies dominated Europe in the 15th century, thanks to commercial privileges – the so-called 'capitulations'– granted to them by the Ottoman sultan. But when the former allies fell out, the Ottomans did not hesitate to extend the same economic privileges to the French, the English and the Dutch over the course of the following two centuries. It was an Ottoman reorientation that proved a decisive turning point in the early mercantilist–capitalist expansion of these rising Western nation-states. By 1914, on the eve of the First World War, Ottoman and Western economies were intertwined to an unprecedented degree.[23]

In modern Turkey, the so-called 'Anatolian Tigers' who have driven Turkey's entrepreneurial economy with their thriving small and medium-sized enterprises in the Anatolian heartland cities (Gaziantep, Malatya, Kayseri and Konya, for instance) are mainly hard-working, devout Muslims, happy that Islam has been brought back into the centre of political and economic life. Most have received little state investment and few subsidies, but from the 1980s they have displayed impressive growth on their own. The European Stability Initiative has coined the term 'Islamic Calvanists' to refer to their Islamic values and their 'green capital'. Fittingly, Bursa – the first Ottoman capital, which also figures among the Anatolian Tiger cities – has long been known by Turks as 'the Green City'. The early Ottomans would undoubtedly have approved.

3
Statecraft and Geography

HISTORIANS TODAY CONTINUE to puzzle over the Ottomans and their success. How did their empire endure for 600 years, till the outbreak of the First World War, under a single, centralized administration encompassing multiple ethnicities and religions? What enabled one Turkmen family to step forward from among the many rival and competing Turkic *beyliks* (emirates) to command, within an astonishingly short period of time, an empire that stretched across three continents and a million square miles?

There were many factors in the Ottomans' favour, including the toughness of their psyche and the inclusivity of their commercial spirit. Another was undoubtedly geography, both physical and strategic. Accustomed as they were to the harsh climate and inhospitable mountains of the Central Asian steppes and the Anatolian plateau, the lands around Söğüt offered welcome respite, with their fertile pastures and mild weather. Its location, on the border of the weakening Byzantine Empire, also gave them an obvious frontier to push against in pursuit of more territory. Osman's first datable victory over the Byzantines came in 1301, but even before that he had taken control of small settlements in the surrounding countryside. He is thought to have died aged 68, of natural causes, before Bursa finally fell in 1326, following a tough nine-year siege, leaving his son Orhan to declare the city as the first Ottoman capital. The capture of Iznik (Byzantine Nicaea), former capital of the Seljuks before they were forced to retreat to Konya, had eluded Osman, despite a two-year siege from 1299. It finally surrendered to Orhan a few decades later, in 1331, after another long siege.

Also important was Christian disunity. A major blow had been struck when, in 1054, the Latin Catholics of Rome branded the Orthodox Byzantines, whose patriarchate was in Constantinople, as schismatic. This rift culminated in the disastrous Fourth Crusade of 1204, in which the Catholic Crusader armies, instead of heading to the Holy Land to recapture Jerusalem, instead diverted to Constantinople and sacked the city. The Crusaders then compounded the ignominy by staying on in occupation of the Byzantine capital until 1261. The bitter taste of that betrayal had driven many Greeks to favour the Turks rather than the Catholics, since it had been made very clear that the Crusades were far more about establishing the supremacy of Rome and the pope than fighting Islam. Many historians have speculated that, had it not been for the Fourth Crusade's fatal weakening and destruction of Constantinople, the Ottomans would not have succeeded in conquering it in 1453. In contrast with the bigotry and persecution displayed by the Latin Catholics towards the Orthodox Christians, the Ottomans protected the Orthodox. 'Better the sultan's turban than the pope's mitre,' the Patriarch Gennadius is quoted as saying, and the Muslim Turks were often seen by the Christians of south-eastern Europe as liberators. The intolerance shown by modern Islamic fundamentalists such as ISIS, Al-Qaeda and the Taliban towards those holding different views to their own runs completely contrary to the religious tolerance shown by

1 Enthronement of Mehmet II in Edirne in 1451, two years before his conquest of Constantinople. It was the Ottoman custom, derived from earlier Turkic traditions, to kiss the corner of the ruler's garment in a sign of homage. Each of his officials would have come forward to do this one by one as part of the ceremony. Miniature dated 1523.

2 Ottoman map of the Maghreb and Middle East, late 16th century, marking Africa, Egypt and the Mediterranean islands like Cyprus, Rhodes and Crete in Ottoman Turkish.

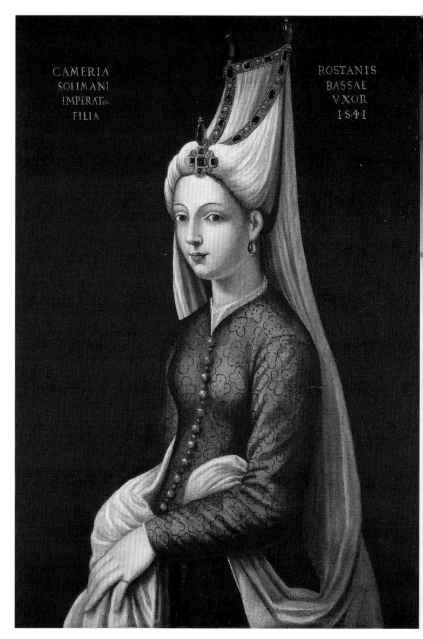

CAMERIA
SOLIMANI
IMPERATor
FILIA

ROSTANIS
BASSAE
VXOR
I·S·4·I

3 Portrait of Princess Mihrimah, daughter of Sultan Süleyman and Roxelana, reputedly the richest woman in the world at the time. She commissioned a range of charitable foundations, some designed by the famed court architect Sinan. After Cristofano dell'Altissimo, Italian school, second half of the 16th century.

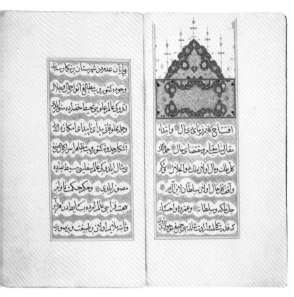

4 Endowment deed of Princess Mihrimah for a mosque complex built by Ottoman court architect Sinan in Üsküdar, dated 1550. It sets out detailed explanations behind the endowment of properties in Anatolia and Rumelia, and elaborates how revenues were to be used to meet the expenses of the complex.

5 Khan As'ad Pasha in Damascus, built in the heart of the Spice Bazaar in 1753 by the powerful Al-'Azem family, as drawn by John Carne on his visit to Syria in 1836. Every notable businessman in Damascus would have rented a room here. Today it is often used as an exhibition space.

6 Mehmet the Conqueror, trilingual, and highly educated, was both widely feared and admired in Europe. He believed that ideal universal rule should embrace both the intellectual and artistic cultures of the lands that he governed, through the mediation of poets, writers, historians, painters, mathematicians and astronomers employed at his court. This painting is attributed to Ottoman artist Shiblizade Ahmed (active 1475–1500).

7 Jewish woman, from a late 18th-century (*c.* 1790) album of Turkish costumes.

8 Chief Rabbi of Istanbul, from a late 18th-century album of Turkish costumes. The Jews in Istanbul were given more freedoms under the Ottomans than in other parts of Europe.

9 Whirling dervish (Mevlevi). The Mevlevis in Konya were more or less contemporary with Ahi Evren, founder of the Ahi Brotherhood, a socio-religious fraternity of craft and trade guilds built on Islamic values that thrived from the 1200s right through till the end of Ottoman rule.

the Muslim Ottomans towards all resident foreign communities. Even as late as 1715, the Ottoman capture of the Morea from the Venetians was felt by the Greeks to be a liberation from the hated Latin Catholics.[1]

It is worth stressing that, for most of Ottoman history, the relationship between the Turks and their non-Muslim subjects – the Greeks and the Armenians, for example – was generally good, going disastrously wrong only in the late 19th and early 20th centuries. There were undoubtedly times when the Turks committed brutal acts – like all imperial powers, Britain included – but these were not motivated by differences of religion, ethnicity or race. They were acts of punishment for perceived betrayal and disloyalty to the Ottoman state. Religious tolerance was an active Ottoman policy. As the historian Caroline Finkel has written: 'The pervasive notion of permanent and irreconcilable division between the Muslim and the Christian worlds at this time is a fiction.'[2] When in 1369 Osman's grandson Murad I moved the Ottoman capital from Bursa to Edirne in Thrace, the Ottomans turned their back on their Seljuk inheritance and established a base from which to challenge the supremacy of Rome and the Austro-Hungarian Empire. When the Hungarians led a crusade blessed by the pope in the 1360s against Christian Bulgaria – because the Bulgarians were Orthodox, not Catholic – frequently forcing them to convert to Catholicism, the Bulgarians welcomed the Ottomans for allowing freedom of worship and offering protection to their religion. The Battle of Kosovo in 1389 – won under Murad I's son Beyazıt I, nicknamed 'the Thunderbolt' – resulted in Kosovo gradually becoming Muslim and in the Ottomans' establishment as a permanent and major power in the heart of Europe.[3] Kosovo remains 95 per cent Muslim today.

As Ottoman military strength increased, clever alliances through marriage were another successful tactic. Orhan married Princess Theodora, daughter of the Emperor John VI, in a splendid ceremony in 1346. Turkmen tradition was oral in these early times (Ottoman history was not written down until the 15th century), leaving us with many unanswerable questions about the historical accuracy of events during the empire's early days. Weddings to prominent Christian women were easy to justify as realpolitik, but when the Ottomans also started to conquer fellow Muslim neighbouring *beyliks* in Anatolia the chroniclers sometimes struggled to explain why this was necessary.

Even the forces of nature are accounted for differently by Byzantine and Ottoman historians. The former cite the huge earthquake of 1354 as the major reason for the weakness of Byzantine towns on the Sea of Marmara and for their fall to the Ottomans, while the Ottoman sources make no mention of it.[4] Some historians believe that the so-called Little Ice Age may have played a role, although climate specialists dispute its exact dates. According to one theory, cooling events began to take place between 1275 and 1300, just when the Ottomans were emerging as a principality in north-west Anatolia, and may even have contributed to the speed of their rise by weakening the Byzantines. Another theory, explored in Chapter 8, is that the Black Death hit the Byzantine city-dwellers much harder than the nomadic Ottomans, for all the same reasons that the COVID-19 pandemic caused more deaths in urban environments across the world than in rural populations.

Exceptionally strong personalities must also have played a part, starting with Ertuğrul, Osman's father, who first brought the tribe west and won the trust of the Seljuk sultan. Osman himself and his son Orhan must also have been natural leaders, given their remarkable achievements, although little is recorded of their characters. By the time of Mehmet the Conqueror (see plate 1), who first came to power in 1444, there are far more sources, and it is evident that this sultan was both widely feared and admired in Europe. A contemporary Venetian described him as:

> Noble in arms, of an aspect inspiring fear rather than reverence, sparing of laughter, a pursuer of knowledge, gifted with princely liberality, stubborn of purpose, bold in all things, as avid for fame as Alexander of Macedon. Every day he has Roman and other histories read to him ... chronicles of the popes, the emperors, the kings of France, the Lombards; he speaks three languages, Turkish, Greek and Slavonic. Diligently he seeks information ... on the Pope, of the Emperor, and how many kings there are in Europe, of which he has a map showing the states and provinces. Nothing gives him greater pleasure than to study the state of the world and the science of war. A shrewd explorer of affairs, he burns with the desire to rule. It is with such a man that we Christians have to deal.[5]

After the Muslim conquest of Constantinople in 1453, the population remained largely Greek; as a result, most official Ottoman documents were written in both Turkish and Greek. There was even a Greek revival after 1714: centred on the Phanar (Fener) quarter that overlooks the Golden Horn, it flourished so greatly under the Ottomans, relying on its own schools and churches, that it became the wealthiest community in the empire. Some of these Phanariotes were made princes of Wallachia and Moldavia under the Ottomans; and when Catherine the Great of Russia tried to woo one of the grandest Greek princes, Alexander Mavrocordato, who was Ottoman prince of Moldavia, to join the Russian side, his polite refusal was: 'It is better that Her Majesty regard me as a friendly Turk, which does not detract from my quality as a Christian, but on the contrary my Christian faith orders me even to be faithful to my Emperor.'[6] The name 'Constantinople' remained the same right down to the 20th century ('Constantinopolis' in Greek, and Turkish 'Qustantiniyya') and, far from being Turkish, as many imagine, 'Istanbul' in fact derives from a corruption of the Greek 'Eistanpolis', meaning 'to the city'.

The dynasty preserved the mindset of a small professional military group gathered round its military leader throughout its entire socio-political structure. Its policy from the outset was dynamic conquest, and the military class was therefore predominant. The janissary corps – the first professional standing army in Europe, which operated under the direct command of the sultan – increased from 1,000 in the 1360s to 5,000 under Beyazıt I (r. 1389–1402).

The capture of the 'Red Apple', as Constantinople was known by the Turks, brought Mehmet the Conqueror immense personal authority. From that point on, he styled himself 'Caesar of the Romans' and 'Sultan of Two Lands and the Khan of Two Seas'. He was now the most powerful sovereign in the Islamic world, able to challenge the Islamic empires of Iran and Egypt.

Mehmet's conquests made the Ottoman Empire a territorially compact unit between the Danube and the Euphrates – a region that would remain its heartland till the 19th century. Such rapid expansion was made possible not only through his powerful artillery, which was in the hands of a janissary army that had now grown even larger, doubling from 5,000 to 10,000 men, but also because of the policy of reconciliation (*istimalet*) that was practised in all newly conquered territories.

Under Mehmet, Constantinople, which had suffered severe neglect in the final years of Byzantine rule, became once again the capital of a great empire, drawing together the best from both eastern and western cultures. Mehmet's son Beyazıt II, for example, negotiated with both Michelangelo and Leonardo da Vinci in 1505 to build a bridge over the Bosphorus; although neither of them ever came to the city, Leonardo's proposals for a giant arch spanning 350 metres (1,148 feet) are preserved in the Topkapı Palace archives. Michelangelo constructed a model of it.[7]

The conquest of Constantinople is always seen as the great landmark in Ottoman history, but the empire's most spectacular expansions in fact came later, under Beyazıt II's son, whom the Turks called 'Selim the Resolute' (r. 1487–1510), who defeated Persia and all of the Arab Near East – a feat that entitled him to add 'caliph' to his titles.

Under Selim the Resolute's successor, Süleyman the Magnificent (r. 1520–66), the Ottoman Empire reached its zenith. Süleyman's epithet, 'Kanuni' ('the Lawmaker'), evoked both the Byzantine emperor Justinian and the Old Testament king Solomon. In a conscious re-enactment of earlier traditions, Süleyman reintroduced Roman-style spectacle into Constantinople, instituting dramatic displays in the Hippodrome. On the occasion of his marriage to the former slave girl Roxelana, gladiatorial-style tournaments were held that featured both Muslim and Christian knights, wild beasts, juggling and acrobatic performances.

As well as representing the peak of Ottoman achievement, Süleyman's reign is also generally taken as marking the beginning of its decline, starting with the sultan's notorious execution of his eldest son, Mustafa, while in the Christian Europe of the period, usually depicted so positively by Western historians, we should remember the terrible Wars of Religion of the 16th and 17th centuries – conflicts between Catholics and Protestants during which an estimated 15 million lives were lost across Europe.

Warfare techniques and army recruitment

The Ottomans were the first to use gunpowder (invented by the Chinese) and heavy artillery on a large scale in European warfare. They also perfected the combined land-and-sea pincer campaign, utilized, for instance, in their capture of Lepanto, in the waters off south-western Greece, from Venice in 1499. They maintained their supremacy over the centuries through warfare and military expansion, relying on a war-based economy and building a sense of unity through martial successes. The highpoint of their expansion northwards came in 1529 with the siege of Vienna, though they failed to capture the city. It was also at Vienna, 150 years later, in 1683, that they suffered their first major defeat.

The Ottomans' highly disciplined soldiers, the janissaries, constituted Europe's first standing army since the Romans and struck fear into the hearts of Western Christians. 'I tremble when I think of what the future must bring when I compare the Turkish system with our own,' wrote Ogier de Busbecq, Habsburg ambassador at the court of Süleyman in 1555. 'One army must prevail and the other be destroyed, for certainly both cannot remain unscathed. On their side are the resources of a mighty empire, strength unimpaired, experience and practice in fighting, a veteran soldiery, habituation to victory, endurance of toil, unity, order, discipline, frugality and watchfulness. On our side is public poverty, private luxury, impaired strength, broken spirit, lack of endurance and training, the soldiers are insubordinate, the officers avaricious; there is contempt for discipline; licence, recklessness, drunkenness and debauchery are rife; and worst of all, the enemy is accustomed to victory, and we to defeat. Can we doubt what the result will be?'[8]

On the *devşirme* system (explained in Chapter 1), which enabled the creation of the janissary corps in the first place, de Busbecq also noted the huge contrast between the Ottoman system and that of the Habsburgs:

In all that great assembly no single man owed his dignity to anything but his personal merits and bravery; no one is distinguished from the rest by his birth, and honour is paid to each man according to the nature of the duty and offices which he discharges ...

In Turkey every man has it in his power to make what he will of the position into which he is born and of his fortune in life. Those who hold the highest posts under the sultan are very often the sons of shepherds and herdsmen, and, so far from being ashamed of their birth, they make it a subject of boasting, and the less they owe to their forefathers and to the accident of birth, the greater is the pride which they feel.

Just as they consider that an aptitude for the arts, such as music or mathematics or geometry, is not transmitted to a son and heir, so they hold that character is not hereditary, and that a son does not necessarily resemble his father, but his qualities are divinely infused into his bodily frame.

Thus, among the Turks, dignities, offices and administrative posts are the rewards of ability and merit; those who are dishonest, lazy and slothful never attain to distinction, but remain in obscurity and contempt. This is why the Turks succeed and are a dominating race and daily extend the bounds of their rule.[9]

Such a meritocracy is hard to achieve even today. Five centuries ago it was unheard of. The *devşirme* boys were carefully observed during their training, so that their individual talents and potential could be spotted. On graduation, they were streamed into one of two fields, the army or the administration, with the brightest earmarked for the higher posts. This created the first ever professional civil service in European history, trained since childhood and completely removed from the vested interests of a landed gentry, tribal ties or rich mercantile families. The arrangement meant that ordinary people from as far away as Scotland could convert to Islam voluntarily in order to enter the service of the Ottoman court and to rise to the top. As the historian Philip Mansel has noted: 'A hundred years ago, might not selected Irish Catholic youths have felt a similar pride, if they had been converted to Protestantism, sent to Eton and then told to govern the British Empire as servants of the Queen Empress?'[10]

The Ottoman state had virtually no controlling aristocracy in its early centuries, thanks to the *devşirme*. An example of the system at its best is provided by Rüstem Pasha, originally a Catholic Croat swineherd from near Sarajevo, who not only rose to become Süleyman the Magnificent's longest serving grand vizier, but also married Süleyman and Roxelana's only daughter, the Princess Mihrimah – then the richest woman in the world. Men often appear to have maintained connections with their home villages after their recruitment, as a few stories reveal. In the case of Rüstem Pasha, Warwick Ball relates how an ordinary Greek sailor would regularly get drunk in the taverns of the Golden Horn every time he was on shore leave, then 'stagger up the hill to the palace of the grand vizier and demand loudly to be let in. There the palace servants had standing orders to allow him in, put him in a room to sleep it off. The following morning the vizier himself would personally invite him to share breakfast and then send him on his way with a purse of money and the parting words: And give my love to the rest of the family.'[11] A 1572 document discovered in the Ottoman archives details a petition from a janissary to the sultan on behalf of his family in Albania.[12] Another grand vizier, Mahmud Pasha, acting on behalf of Mehmet the Conqueror, negotiated a settlement in favour of the Serbs in 1457: the opposite number with whom he negotiated was his own brother, the prime minister Michael Angelović.[13]

Possibly the most talented grand vizier of all was Sokullu Mehmet Pasha ('Mehmet from Sokolovići' or 'Sokolac', a town in Serbia), architect of a new world order. He was recruited to the *devşirme* system from a Serbian village, rising to become high admiral of the Ottoman fleet and later the grand vizier at the empire's peak. Once in power, he revived the Serbian Orthodox Church and appointed his brother Macarios as its first patriarch (1557–71), one of many examples in which *devşirme* boys used their power to favour their former native towns and cities. Sokullu Mehmet also commissioned Sinan, the court architect, to build a fine, eleven-arched bridge over the Drina near his hometown in Višegrad (the subject of Ivo Andrić's famous novel *The Bridge over the Drina*, published in 1945). Like Rüstem Pasha, Sokullu Mehmet also commissioned Sinan to build a mosque in his own name (both are gems of Istanbul architecture) using the Islamic religious endowment system known as *waqf* (see pp. 32, 35).

Refugee policies

In another remarkable difference with the Ottomans' approach to different communities, and therefore to their acceptance and welcome of refugees, the Europeans had a tendency to evict communities based on the perceived ethnic superiority of one group over another. The expulsion of religious minorities was a common feature of the European landscape from the late Middle Ages and was based on early European efforts to build nation-states with a shared ethno-religious background. Minorities who were deemed to be threatening to the dominant group, or religious communities that did not follow the established majority religion, were cast out.[14]

The powerful medieval pope Innocent III, who claimed supremacy over all Europe's kings, forbade Christians from living, working or trading with Jews. The English expelled their Jews in 1291, the French in 1343, and many German states in the early 1400s. Renaissance Europe in the 16th century expelled thousands of Jews, not only from Spain and Portugal but also from Italy, the Netherlands and elsewhere. The Ottoman approach, by contrast, was based on the confident notion that Islam was indisputably the superior religion.[15] The Ottomans' tolerance of Jewish and Christian communities followed religious tenets as laid down in the Qur'an, combined with a dose of pragmatic economic and political realism. Their strategy ensured Muslim dominance, and made conversion to Islam politically and economically attractive. This was the main reason why so many Christian communities withered over the centuries in the Muslim lands on the eastern and southern shores of the Mediterranean, sometimes even to extinction.

In the middle of the 15th century a rabbi wrote from Istanbul to his Jewish brethren back in Spain:

Here in the land of the Turks we have nothing to complain of.
We possess great fortunes; much gold and silver are in our hands.

We are not oppressed with heavy taxes, and our commerce is free and unhindered. Everything is cheap and every one of us lives in peace and freedom. Here the Jew is not compelled to wear a yellow star as a badge of shame, as is the case in most of Germany, where even wealth and great fortune are a curse for a Jew because he therewith arouses jealousy among the Christians and they devise all kind of slander against him to rob him of his gold. Arise my brethren, gird up your loins, collect all your forces and come to us.[16]

In 1492 the Spanish Sephardim, 'reviled by the Inquisition', were stripped of their wealth and possessions and banished from their homeland by Ferdinand and Isabella of Spain. In all, about 100,000 of these Jewish refugees set sail for Istanbul, where Sultan Beyazıt II had ordered that they be allowed unimpeded entry. The Jews in Istanbul were given more freedoms under the Ottomans than in other parts of Europe (see plates 7 and 8). As a result, from the 16th century onwards the Ottoman Empire had the largest Jewish communities in the world, with Istanbul and Thessalonica their biggest centres. It was the same for the Greeks, who also enjoyed cultural and religious rights. Along with other non-Muslims, all the Sephardim had to do was to pay the poll tax, a sum that was lower than their tax obligations in Catholic Spain, and to pledge obedience to the Ottoman state. The sultan is said to have mocked the Spanish monarch's lack of wisdom: 'You call Ferdinand a wise king, he who makes his land poor and ours rich!'

Indeed, anti-Semitism baffled the Ottomans. When occasional anti-Jewish riots broke out in Constantinople, they were invariably stirred up not by Muslims, but by Christians accusing the Jews of the ritual kidnapping, murder and eating of Christian children. Jews enjoyed the protection of the Ottomans against Christian persecution till the end of the 19th century, and Jews remain the largest minority in Istanbul today.

Charitable giving was also an essential tenet of Ottoman statecraft. During the 1845–52 Irish Potato Famine, for instance, which saw 1 million dead and the mass exodus of 1 million more, the Ottoman sultan declared that he was ready to send £10,000 to help Ireland's farmers. Queen Victoria intervened, however, and asked that the sultan send no more than £1,000, since she herself had sent only £2,000. He complied, to spare her embarrassment, but in secret also sent five ships laden with food. The English courts tried to block the shipment, but the food arrived and was delivered by the Ottoman sailors. The story is the subject of an Irish–Turkish film called *Famine*, released in 2021,[17] with profits donated to UNICEF.

Russian meddling and Ottoman decline

It was the Russian imperial agenda that caused the most damage to the Ottoman Empire. Unable to expand further into Europe – or, for that matter, into Asia – the Russians saw the Ottoman Empire as their natural route to expansion. Specifically, they wanted Constantinople, the Dardanelles and the Bosphorus Strait in order to gain access to the Mediterranean. They aimed to dismember the empire, dividing it between themselves, the Habsburgs and a renascent Byzantium. Historically the Western powers tended to oppose Russian expansion (as in the Crimean War, for example), preferring an equilibrium between Russia and the Ottomans, but they were sympathetic to the argument that Christians within the empire were oppressed. The Russians repeatedly invaded Ottoman territories, capturing lands in both Europe and Asia. They forced the creation of an independent Bulgaria, Serbia and Romania by defeating the

Ottomans in wars they themselves had initiated.[18] Russia would then demand reparations for its wartime losses – demands that were often mediated by the European powers to soften the blow to the 'Sick Man of Europe'. The Russians dispossessed and ejected the native populations of Circassia and Abkhazia in the Caucasus, forcing the Ottomans to take in more than 800,000 Caucasian peoples at great human and civil cost. A further 900,000 Turks were also forced out of these border lands into the Ottoman Empire, which then had to find food and shelter for them at a time when the existing population was already poor.[19] Much of the economic and military disaster that constantly threatened the Ottomans in the 19th century was therefore due to the machinations of the Russian tsars.

The Ottoman Empire continued to shrink territorially as one after another its European provinces, with European encouragement and support, rebelled and seceded. In 1850 some 50 per cent of all Ottoman subjects lived in the Balkans, yet by 1906 the remaining Balkan provinces made up just 20 per cent of the Ottoman population.[20]

The Ottomans, however, had been the first to mount an organized response to a mass influx of forced migrants. In fact, the 19th century was sometimes labelled the 'century of refuge' for this reason. The Ottomans issued a Refugee Code in 1857 in response to the arrival of massive numbers of migrant Muslim Tatars forced from the Crimea, but there were also refugees from other regions on the borders with Russia. Migrants, who were regularly pushed out of their homes with no time to prepare, often had no option but to travel with little more than the clothes on their backs and a few possessions piled into ox-carts. Before the promulgation of the Refugee Code, their survival depended on the kindness of local people and municipal authorities. Many died on the road from starvation and disease. As the sheer scale of the influx became clear, localized and decentralized Ottoman organizations were set up to help and resettle the migrants. Local towns and cities opened up their mosques and churches to shelter and feed the exiles. Various local authorities levied additional municipal taxes per head to help in funding their feeding and clothing.

The Ottoman policy was to swiftly disperse and integrate its forced migrants, providing each 'immigrant' family with an initial amount of capital and plots of state land so that they could start life anew as agricultural workers. Families who applied for land in the Ottoman province of Rumelia (literally, 'the land of the Romans', the area of south-eastern Europe that would later be known as the Balkans) were granted exemptions from taxation and conscription obligations for a period of six years. If they chose to continue their migration into Anatolia and Greater Syria, their exemptions were extended for a period of twelve years. In either case, the new immigrants had to agree to cultivate the land and not to sell or leave it for twenty years. Of course, the policy was not entirely disinterested, as Ottoman reformers were keen to see the largely depopulated Syrian provinces revived by new immigration following centuries of maladministration, war and famine, and several plague pandemics.[21] The twenty-year prohibition on onward sale also meant that these newcomers were relieved of pressure from 19th-century property developers, since there was a kind of lien on the property.

The forced migrants were also promised freedom of religion and were permitted to construct their own places of worship. News of the Refugee Code spread widely along the frontier zones and the Ottomans even advertised in European newspapers for immigrant families wishing to settle as farmers in the Levant. As the number of requests from forced migrants and potential immigrants for plots of state land rose, the Ottomans set up a refugee commission in 1860 (the Ottoman Commission for the General Administration of Immigration) under the Ministry of Trade. The commission had the responsibility for integrating not only the Muslim Tatars and Circassians fleeing from lands conquered by the Russians north and west of the Black Sea, but also the thousands of non-Muslim immigrant farmers and political leaders from Hungary, Bohemia and Poland, Cossacks from Russia and Bulgarians from the Balkans.[22]

The population ruled over by the Ottoman Empire was divided, according to its own philosophy of statecraft, into two main groups: the *askeri* (from the Arabic for 'soldier', 'army' or 'enlisted men'), who formed the military or administrative class and were officially exempted from all taxation; and the *reaya* (literally 'the flock') – the merchants, artisans and peasants who pursued productive activities and therefore paid taxes. The Ottoman word *reaya* comes from the Arabic root *ra'a* meaning 'to tend, guard, protect and care for' (the same word is used for 'parish' in a Christian context). *Raayi*, the derived noun, means a shepherd or a pastor. According to this philosophy, the ruler, in accordance with ancient Oghuz tradition, was a shepherd protecting his flock, and the Ottoman sultans strove to show to their subjects that their primary concern was to protect them against all kinds of injustice. In case of conscious or unconscious bias, European sources interpreted the concept of the *reaya* as 'the herd', with obvious negative overtones. The masterly *Bridge over the Drina*, published in 1945, which helped its Yugoslav author win the Nobel Prize for Literature in 1961, perpetuates the notion of the word *reaya* as referring to Christian serfs, when in reality it applied equally to subjects of any religion, including Muslims. In 1992 over 3,000 Muslims were ethnically cleansed in Višegrad by Christian Serbs. Many were thrown off the bridge, causing the manager of the hydroelectric plant downstream to complain that their bloated bodies were clogging up his dam. When it was drained for repairs in 2010, their remains were found. DNA samples showed that they ranged from 94 to just 3 years of age.[23]

Ottoman statecraft in many ways represented the complete opposite of modern nationalism. Their system of government tolerated, indeed encouraged, difference among peoples. At the heart of the Ottoman Empire, a person's sense of belonging was not based just on their physical birthplace, but specifically included the wider social community of origin.[24] It was 'rooted in the connections and links between and among a specific group of people as much as, if not more than, in a territory. The empire upon which such identities were based – the Ottoman Empire – came to an end with the First World War.'[25]

4
Religious Values

ONE OF THE most striking aspects of the early Ottomans was the constant presence of dervishes (Muslim holy men) among them, both as fighters and as spiritual guides. But alongside Muslim holy men, wandering Christian monks also chose to join the Ottomans in these fluctuating frontier lands, together with a whole range of nomads, fighting men, migrants and pilgrims.[1]

The dervish connection was deeply embedded from the start. The Ottoman chroniclers tell us that Osman, when he was the *bey* of the Kayı tribe, married the daughter of Sheikh Edebali, a highly respected local dervish and Sufi mystic. While staying overnight in Sheikh Edebali's house, Osman is said to have had his prophetic dream foretelling his foundation of the Ottoman dynasty, a story first recorded in written form in the 15th century:

> He saw that a moon arose from the holy man's breast and came to sink in his own breast. A tree then sprouted from his navel and its shade encompassed the world. Beneath this shade there were mountains, and streams flowed forth from the foot of each mountain. Some people drank from these running waters, others watered gardens, while yet others caused fountains to flow. When Osman awoke he told the story to the holy man, who said 'Osman, my son,

congratulations, for God has given the imperial office to
you and your descendants and my daughter Malhun shall be
your wife.'[2]

Up till that point, the sheikh had opposed the marriage.
Malhun, Osman's love match according to Ottoman tradition,
went on to bear his first son, Orhan (who became the second
sultan on Osman's death in 1323/24), and five other children.
Sheikh Edebali himself was the local leader of a movement
called the Ahi Brotherhood ('Ahi' derives from the Arabic
for 'my brother', *akhi*), a socio-religious fraternity of craft and
trade guilds built on Islamic values that thrived from the
1200s right through till the end of Ottoman rule. The members
could be from any profession – tailors or tanners, butchers
or bakers – but all had to abide by the same rules, progressing from assistants to apprentices to qualified workmen to
masters. They would achieve the level of 'Ahi', the highest level
of skill, only after years of experience and training. The various
initiation ceremonies had a strongly religious flavour, featur-
ing prayers and recitations from the Qur'an, making them very
similar to the progress a Sufi had to make to reach the highest
level of authority in his Sufi lodge. Honesty was paramount:
it was obligatory for members to offer customers the highest
possible quality at the fairest possible price. Charity was also
essential, and adherents gave free accommodation and food to
the poor at all times. The early influence of the Ahi movement
on Osman and his successors was crucial to the founding principles of the Ottoman state they set out to establish.

The founder of the fraternity, Ahi Evren, is believed to have
died fighting the Mongols in 1261, aged 93. A leatherworker
from Iran, he was also a well-versed scholar thanks to his education, acquired from prominent Muslim teachers in Baghdad

and Khorasan. His organization helped the many displaced Turkmens fleeing from the Mongol invasion, giving them food and work while simultaneously teaching them religious values. Ahi Evren organized guilds for thirty-two different professions, shaping a highly influential economic and social system that formed the foundation of the moral tenets of both the Seljuk and the Ottoman empires. In addition to writing twenty books across his lifetime, he was also instrumental in organizing the Ahis into a fighting force against the Mongol incursions into Anatolia.

Evren's wife, Fatma, set up a similar network for women, called the 'Sisters of Rum' (Anatolia was known as 'Rum' at that time, meaning 'Eastern Rome'), which included professions such as carpet-weaving and clothing manufacture. In Bursa, Konya and Kayseri the network had its own meeting places, which can still be seen, and the women were actively engaged in social care, looking after orphans or elderly women who had lost their own families.

The Ottomans took women's rights very seriously and, from the 15th century onwards, women of all classes and all religions had the option to take their grievances to court all across the empire. Court records show that women from all territories were frequent plaintiffs, and that Orthodox Christian women flocked to the Islamic courts in such numbers that Christian clergy became alarmed.[3] Some Turkish traditions were not just grounded in Islamic law, but had roots further back in their Central Asian nomadic ways. Women in such nomadic societies were involved by necessity in all levels of tribal life, actively participating as income-earners through their rug workshops but also even fighting alongside their menfolk if the situation demanded and if the safety of the tribe was at stake.

Legends of the Amazons are thought to date back to these fighting Central Asian tribeswomen.[4] They had a toughness that is apparent even today, when Turkish women play active roles as breadwinners and business owners across the country.

Images of women in the Ottoman Empire have been distorted by Western fascination with the harem and lascivious tales of concubines and sultans. In practice, however, only about 2 per cent of marriages in the empire were polygamous, and the imperial harem was a one-off, a unique institution that was not representative of how Ottoman society worked in general. Where polygamy was practised, it usually involved the taking of two wives, not the four permitted in the Qur'an, and it was often used in traditional Muslim societies as a good way of looking after widows or orphans who would otherwise have no support and nowhere to live. In most Christian European societies, the solution was usually the convent or the asylum for the elite, and the street for the rest. Fantasies surrounding the harem also perpetuated the myth in Western societies that Ottoman women were more secluded than their Christian European counterparts. It is also worth remembering that, throughout pre-modern Europe, all women wore some form of head covering, be they Muslim, Catholic, Protestant, Orthodox or Jewish.

The Ahi Brotherhood came to prominence at much the same time as other mystic Sufi groups in Anatolia. The Mevlevis in Konya were more or less contemporary with Ahi Evren, while the Bektashis had been founded a little earlier by Hacı Bektash Veli, who settled in central Anatolia. The Ahis gradually declined, especially after the janissaries had been disbanded, since many of their members had belonged to these forces (the fighting dervish tradition again). By 1923, when the Turkish Republic was declared, there were hardly any left. In Kırşehir, the small city in central Turkey where Ahi Evren died, an annual festival is still held today, organized by local chambers of commerce, to remember the medieval fraternity. At its close, an exemplary tradesman is rewarded as 'Ahi of the year'.

The earliest extant document of the Ottoman state showed that Orhan, son of Osman, granted land east of Iznik to a dervish lodge in 1324 – proof that Islam was part of the Ottoman public identity from the start. Orhan styled himself as 'Champion of the Faith' and referred to his late father, Osman, as 'Glory of the Faith'.[5] Dervish lodges attracted settlement and secured the loyalty of local people, since they symbolized popular forms of Islam open to all. It was a Sunni Muslim tradition that had already flourished across Anatolia under the Seljuk sultans. Orhan founded many theological colleges during his lifetime, and the Ottoman sultans who followed him continued the tradition. All of them were affiliated with one or another of the dervish orders in a demonstration of how 'coexistence and compromise between different manifestations of religious belief and practice is one of the abiding themes of Ottoman history'.[6]

The conversion of local people was a gradual process, taking place over several centuries through a steady but incremental Islamization and Turkification,[7] aided no doubt by political and economic considerations. Well before Osman, the title commonly assumed by Turkmen chieftains was *ghazi*, meaning one who conducts *ghaza* (Arabic *ghazwa*; a word derived from the Arabic root for 'raiding'). It was widely used even in Seljuk times to mean 'war for the faith' and can be considered a synonym for jihad or holy war, except that in the 14th century this term did not carry the anti-Christian baggage of today. Jihad was not a specific religious injunction and meant no more than that it was the duty of all Muslims to fight against non-believers for the sake of their faith. Historians generally agree that the Ottoman conquests were not victories for Islam as part of some kind of holy war, but rather a 'predatory confederacy' of Muslims and Christians alike, whose goal was booty, plunder and slaves, 'no matter the rhetoric used by its rulers'.[8] It was the later Ottoman chroniclers who sought to emphasize a specifically Islamic character for the early Turkmen tribesmen, because it suited the politics of the times, when most battles were being fought against the Christian states of the Balkans. It is the same with recent Turkish TV series such as *Diriliş: Ertuğrul*, which are highly entertaining and go to great lengths to achieve historical accuracy, using Turkmen tents, costumes, props and hairstyles, but the Islamic fervour of the fighters – which suits the political agenda of the current president of Turkey, Recip Tayyib Erdoğan – seems much overplayed. The reality is that Turkmen Muslims were in the minority in these early Ottoman armies, which required large numbers of non-Muslim fighters to meet their manpower shortage.

Orhan's Christian wife, known to the Turks as 'Nilüfer Hatun' after her marriage, was allowed to remain a practising Christian while at the same time being given the power to endow Muslim religious establishments.[9] So readily did the Christian powers form alliances with the Ottomans that, according to many historians, their entry into Europe could almost be described as more by invitation than invasion. The writer and historian Patrick Kinross noted how the Ottoman Turks were 'well entrenched with more than a foothold in Europe, not as enemies but as allies of Byzantium, with a Sultan who was son-in-law of one Emperor, brother-in-law of the other – and also son-in-law of the neighbouring tsar of Bulgaria'.[10] The latter is a reference to Murad I, who married Kera Tamara, daughter of the Bulgarian emperor. She remained a Christian and was buried in Bursa alongside Murad I in 1389. One small group of Ottomans remained so loyal to the Byzantines that they were even inside Constantinople in 1453, fighting against Mehmet the Conqueror. Kinross concluded that 'The year 1453 marked a synthesis, not a conquest.'[11]

Christianity, as well as Islam, was a religion that originated east of Europe, and there is no reason why Islam could therefore not be considered a European religion in the same way as Christianity. Both had been imported many centuries ago, with far more interaction between them than is widely realized. Muslim Europe, after all, still exists, in spite of many attempts to eradicate it: countries including Albania, Bosnia and Herzegovina and Kosovo still have majority Muslim populations, North Macedonia is one-third Muslim, and the Serbian city of Novi Pazar remains 80 per cent Muslim.

There are many examples of why the common Western narrative of age-old Muslim–Christian confrontation is so misleading and inaccurate, a distortion of history that has consequences for today's perceptions of Islam and Muslims in the West. The Ottoman sultan Beyazıt ('the Thunderbolt'), for example, had large numbers of Christian soldiers fighting in his army, and his wife was a Christian Serb. His eldest son was called Isa (Jesus), and Serb allies fought alongside him at Kosovo. Several warrior families who fought with the Ottomans and helped them expand in the Balkans were Christians who converted to Islam, such as the prominent Serb Malkoviç family. When the Ottomans annexed Hungary in 1526, the Ottoman forces included a huge contingent of Christian Greeks, Bulgarians and Bosnians who fought of their own accord. Over one-third of the so-called 'Turkish' forces who occupied Budapest were in fact

Ottoman Greeks, and in Hungary overall the ethnic Turks are estimated to have made up as little as 5 per cent of the invading soldiers.[12] It is also worth mentioning that small trading communities of Muslims had existed in Hungary well before the Ottoman conquest, though most were wiped out before the Ottomans arrived.

Beyazıt's Christian allies played a particularly useful role in his wars against rival Turkish *beyliks* in Anatolia, where it was harder for him to employ Muslim armies against Muslims. Ironically, therefore, the extension of Ottoman power into Anatolia, east of Constantinople, was carried out by Christian allies of the Ottomans, attacking from the European side – the complete opposite of the popular Western perception.[13] It is reminiscent of how Greek writers hijacked the Macedonian legacy when they omitted to mention the Macedonian Alexander the Great's brutal suppression of the Greeks, casting him instead as a Greek hero.[14]

In spite of such evidence, Western sources were adamant in conceptualizing the Ottoman Empire as an Asian state, which is why, in the context of the Balkans, they argued so fiercely against the dominant culture and heritage of the Ottomans, insisting instead on the priority of local origins for such things as house design, cuisine and lifestyle. Even the most casual observer can see that these things are clearly of Ottoman origin.

The *millet* system

Ottoman law did not recognize notions of ethnicity or citizenship. All across the empire there was a thorough mix of ethnicities and religions, especially in Ottoman Europe. In some cases a village might be made up entirely of one ethnic or religious group and yet be adjacent to a village of another group, while in other cases the inhabitants of villages and small towns came from a number of ethnic and religious backgrounds. It was therefore impossible to manage these very diverse peoples on the basis of territoriality.

A Muslim of whatever ethnic background enjoyed exactly the same rights and privileges as any other Muslim. The various sects of Islam – be they Sunni, Shi'a or whatever – had no official status and were all considered part of the Muslim *millet* (from the Arabic *milla*, meaning 'religious community'). Only the Druze enjoyed a type of autonomy; they were considered heretics by both Sunni and Shi'ite Muslims, since they had their own sacred book and law.

Under the Ottoman *millet* system, all populations were recorded in the tax register according to their religion, and not in ethnic or linguistic categories. Muslims within the empire could therefore be Turks, Arabs, Kurds, Albanians, Bosnians, Circassians or others. Jews were mainly Sephardic, descendants of those who had been given refuge after their expulsion from Spain and Portugal, but there were also many Mizrahi (Oriental) Jews. Members of the Christian *millet* were mainly Orthodox and consisted of Greeks, Serbs and Bulgarians in the Balkans, and Arabs in Palestine and Syria. The Armenian Orthodox had their own *millet*, and others, such as the Assyrians and the Roman Catholics, were added later, but only if the Ottomans were satisfied that they genuinely constituted a separate *millet*, otherwise it could result in intra-Christian friction and therefore civil disorder. The Greek Orthodox, for example, opposed the granting of separate *millet* status to the Melkites, Byzantine Rite Catholics from Antioch, Syria.

The Ottomans instituted the *millet* system as an extension of the standard administrative practice. Each *millet* was allowed to manage its own internal affairs and call on its own community's leaders: the Ottomans had a laissez-faire attitude to their internal concerns as long as they paid their taxes. They were allowed to establish and maintain their own places of worship, and to manage their own educational institutions, with the curriculum and language determined by each community. They could set up their own welfare institutions, which were supported and financed by internal taxes they collected from their own community members. They had their own courts to adjudicate on family and civil matters such as marriage, divorce, inheritance and financial transactions, but individuals also had the right to bring their cases to an Islamic court if they felt it might produce a verdict more in their favour than their own community court.

Under such a system there was relative segregation, owing to separate schools promoting each community's own language, culture and customs, but at the same time there was considerable mixing via professional and commercial fields. Physicians, bankers, merchants and craftsmen were particularly well represented among the minority communities, and through their professional and commercial interactions with the Ottoman elite they were often multilingual.[15] This system contrasted strongly with what the modern Turkish Republic instituted under Atatürk in the 20th century, whereby Kurdish language rights, for example, were denied. Kurdish radio stations and media were banned, and everyone was forced to become purely Turkish in the interests of what Atatürk saw as the necessary creation of a homogeneous nationalistic state.

In Ottoman times, of course, it would be wrong to suggest that relations between the religious communities were harmonious at all times. The system did, after all, always favour

Muslims over other *millets*, which could sometimes lead to rivalry and resentment. Christians and Jews paid higher taxes than Muslims and were considered second-class citizens, yet inter-communal violence was extremely rare right through to the 17th and 18th centuries. Relations broke down dramatically only in the 19th century, as in the 1860 massacre of wealthy Christians in the old city of Damascus by Druze peasants, for instance – a disaster whose roots lay more in economic grievances than in religious fervour.

But with the growing influence of Europe among the Ottoman Christian minorities, especially among the French missionary schools, came new revolutionary ideas of equality and liberty connected to the rise of nationalism. This was coupled with the rapid spread of separatist movements in the Balkans, supported by both the Russian and the Habsburg empires.[16] In an attempt to meet these challenges, between 1839 and 1876 the Ottoman governing elite introduced sweeping reforms known as the Tanzimat Charter (*tanzimat* is an Arabic word meaning 'the reorganizations') to modernize all aspects of the administration of the empire along the European model. Great strides were made in turning the Ottoman Empire into a rival to its European contemporaries, so that by the end of the 19th century, for example, Damascus had been restructured, its major roads widened and extended, a tramline built to connect the centre to the suburbs, and railways and a telegraph services set up to connect it to other major cities.[17] The Ottoman government sought to reassure its minorities that their future lay within their empire rather than in the formation of small, independent successor states.

By 1840 the Ottoman state had introduced legal reforms based on European codes that implemented the principle of equality of all before the law. Out of the 125 deputies present at the first Ottoman Parliament in Istanbul (1876), there were 77 Muslims, 44 Christians and 4 Jews – a diversity perhaps unique in the history of multi-ethnic empires.[18]

Even before that, in 1830, Sultan Mahmud II had declared: 'I distinguish among my subjects, Muslims in the mosque, Christians in the church and Jews in the synagogue, but there is no difference among them in any other way. My affection and sense of justice for all of them is strong and they are indeed my children.'[19] One year earlier, in 1829, Ottoman law had set out to minimize visible differences between males by making them all wear the fez, with the result that all government employees now looked the same; different turbans and robes of honour were gone. Only religious clerics of all faiths were exempted.

In 1876 the first written constitution in Ottoman history was promulgated, establishing a limited monarchy and stating that all Osmanlis were equal before the law 'without distinction as to religion'. Throughout the Tanzimat period a series of decrees and edicts raised the status of Christians in the empire. They were given better access to education, government and military service, but the changes came in piecemeal, and many would argue that they were too slow to be implemented, despite the goodwill and intentions of the Ottoman statesmen and lawmakers.[20]

All Ottoman rulers from Selim the Resolute onwards took the title of both 'sultan' and 'caliph', to show that they represented the combined role of secular ruler and Islamic leader. Their approach recalls an earlier dynasty of Tabgach Turk kings in China, the Northern Wei, who were the first to co-opt the religious authority of Buddha into their secular power structures, erecting giant statues of Buddha alongside themselves, just as another Turk dynasty did a short time later with the now destroyed Bamiyan Buddhas in Afghanistan.[21] In Constantinople all these traditions are represented, and no other city in world history has bridged so many civilizations or brought so many cultural strands together (see plate 10).

The Byzantine Christian obsession with holy relics was continued under the Ottomans, and to this day the Topkapı Palace Museum displays Muslim relics such as the mantle of the Prophet, and his sword, to project the Ottoman claim to be the greatest Islamic rulers on earth. They also retained the Greek name of Hagia Sophia (Turkish 'Ayasofya') after the church's conversion into a mosque, both in 1453 and again in 2020.

Protection of persecuted religions was an active policy, and at its height the empire embraced a multitude of ethnicities. Even a Hindu quarter was recorded in 16th-century Constantinople, complete with temple and *ghat*.[22] Hungarian and Transylvanian Calvinists, Silesian Protestants and Russian Old Believers were all given sanctuary in Ottoman Turkey. Polish refugees were welcomed after the partition of Poland in 1795 and after the failed 1848 revolution, as were Hungarian migrants. After Russia occupied the Caucasus in the 1860s, some 600,000 Circassians, Chechens and other Russian Muslims escaping Russian religious persecution fled to the Ottoman Empire, and they remain in distinct communities across the Middle East to this day.[23]

To a large extent, modern Turkey has continued this policy by absorbing Balkan Muslims in the early 20th century, welcoming Kirghiz refugees from Soviet-occupied Afghanistan in the 1980s, and opening their doors since 2011 to some 4 million Syrian refugees fleeing the ongoing Syrian civil war. Most of the Syrians were Sunni Muslims fleeing conscription into President Assad's armed forces, where they would have been compelled to fight against their fellow countrymen. Syria is nominally secular but is roughly 70 per cent Sunni Muslim, whereas the ruling Assad family is from the Alawi sect, which forms 15 per cent of the population. Alawism is a branch of Twelver Shi'a Islam, found predominantly in Iran, Iraq and Bahrain.

There is still a Shi'a minority in Turkey today, which represents roughly 1 per cent of the population of 80 million; more significant are the Alevis (distinct from Syria's Alawis), who make up 15–20 per cent of the populace. The founder of Alevism was Hacı Bektash, a 13th-century Sufi mystic, originally from Khorasan, who is credited with combining Sufi beliefs and practices with those of Shi'ism. Very popular and influential with the early Ottomans, the order had close ties with the janissaries, the elite infantry corps of the Ottoman army. Their lodges were widespread across Anatolia and in the southern Balkans, where there were many converts of Eastern Orthodox origin, especially Albanians, northern Greeks, Macedonians and Bulgarians. When the janissary corps was abolished in 1826, the Bektashi order was banned throughout the empire, but it slowly regained in popularity after the 1839–76 Tanzimat reforms until it was banned again, along with all Sufi orders, by Atatürk in 1925.

As a result, the Bektashi order moved to Albania, where it flourished until the Second World War, when the Communists took over, executing several *babas* (religious leaders – a term of respect derived from the Turkish for 'father'). Enver Hoxha closed all *tekkes* (lodges) and banned religious practice in 1967. Between 1944 and 1967, Albania's 2,000-plus mosques, *tekkes*, churches and monasteries were destroyed as part of Hoxha's drive to create an atheist state. The ban was rescinded in 1990 and the order gradually rebuilt itself. Today the Bektashis have their headquarters in Albania's capital, Tirana, and around one-fifth of Albania's Muslim population continues to claim a connection with the Bektashi order; lodges are spread all over the country once more. However, Albania's Ottoman heritage has been all but erased, even though some thirty Albanians served as grand viziers to the sultan. The Albanian history syllabus covers the 500 years of Ottoman rule in just two lessons, and the bijoux wooden-timbered Ottoman houses of towns such as Berat and Gijirokastër are treated as tourist assets, with little attempt to link them back to their Ottoman origins.[24] Skanderbeg (1405–1468), on the other hand – the Albanian feudal lord and military commander who led a rebellion against the Ottomans – is idealized as a hero and widely commemorated in public statues.

There are also important Bektashi communities in Kosovo and Macedonia, especially in the city of Tetovo, where the Arabati Baba Tekke lodge survives. It is, however, today the subject of a dispute between Saudi-sponsored Salafis and local Bektashis, who display photos of Ali and his sons, Hassan and Hussain, at the *tekke* – anathema to the Sunni traditionalists. Under the Communist Yugoslavs, the lodge was turned into a tourist complex, complete with disco.[25] The tombs of prominent Bektashis serve as pilgrimage sites in Bulgaria, while in modern Turkey there are still active *tekkes* in Istanbul, Ankara and Izmir. There is even a large Bektashi lodge active in Detroit, first established in 1954. In total, there are estimated to be over 7 million Bektashis around the world today. UNESCO declared 2021 to be the 'Year of Haji Bektash Veli' to commemorate the 750th anniversary of the mystic's death, naming him as the greatest Turkish philosopher of the 13th century. A document prepared by UNESCO describes his philosophy as founded on 'humanity, human rights and social equality', noting that he counselled for humankind 'to be modest, to purify his soul, to mature, to abstain from show[ing] off and to be full of love of God'.[26]

Ironically, while the Ottomans were considered too Muslim for Europe, they were thought, from the 18th century onwards, to be not Muslim enough by the puritanical Wahhabis of Saudi Arabia. The role of the Ottomans as protectors of Islam's holy places and of the pilgrimage route or Hajj was central to their credibility in Arab Muslim lands, but not a single one of the Ottoman sultans ever performed the lifetime obligation of undertaking the pilgrimage to Mecca.

5
Scientific and Industrial Innovations

SCIENTIFIC DISCOVERY HAS been a feature of the Middle East since the earliest history of humankind. From the phonetic alphabet to scientific algorithms, numerous significant inventions have emerged from a region that sits, geo-graphically, at the very heart of the inhabited world, at the intersection of three of its five continents and two of its three oceans.[1] Small wonder, then, that throughout history the Middle East should also have been the arena for competing forces – something that quickly becomes clear from the list of ambitious leaders who have sought to dominate the region, from Alexander the Great, Julius Caesar, Hulagu and Tamerlane, to Mehmet the Conqueror and Napoleon.

Competition provides the driver for new discoveries, and while it used to be a widely held view in the West that the Islamic golden age of science ended in 1258, when the Mongols under Hulagu destroyed Baghdad and its irrigation channels, the much-overlooked reality is that scientific activity continued under the Ottomans, sponsored by the Ottoman court. Their specialist fields were advanced mathematics, astronomy, philosophy, geography and chemistry.

Astronomy

One of the most prominent Ottoman scientists was the Damascus-born Taqi al-Din, who died in Istanbul in 1585 aged 59. A polymath who authored more than ninety books, he was invited by Murad III to build an observatory in Istanbul, from where he studied the Great Comet of 1577. He was appointed chief astronomer to the sultan in 1571, following twenty years of study in Cairo. One of his papers on optics is now in the Bodleian Library in Oxford, a result of the 17th-century practice, widespread in European circles, of collecting Arabic manuscripts. William Laud – archbishop of Canterbury, chancellor of Oxford University and founder of the Laudian Professorship of Arabic – commanded every ship returning from the Levant to bring at least one Arabic manuscript back as an aid to Western research. Istanbul was a common source for such highly valued manuscripts. Taqi al-Din's manuscript discusses the structure of light, the relationship between light and colour, and diffusion and global refraction.

The observatory in Tophane (see plate 11), Istanbul, was one of the largest in the world and is often compared to the contemporary Uraniborg observatory, operated by the Danish nobleman and astronomer Tycho Brahe, whose project was likewise fully funded by a government for research purposes, a rarity at the time. Like Taqi al-Din, Tycho Brahe recorded his observations of the 1577 Great Comet visible over all of Europe and, also like his Ottoman counterpart, he fell foul of the politics of the day after a disagreement with his patron, the Danish king, which led to his observatory being destroyed – the same fate that befell the observatory at Tophane. Murad III saw the comet as a bad omen for his war against the Safavids and blamed Taqi al-Din for the plague that was spreading at the time. Unlike its Istanbul counterpart, however, the Uraniborg observatory has now been excavated and its foundations and gardens restored.

As well as the observatory itself, where he had sixteen assistants, Taqi al-Din, like Tycho Brahe, had groups of highly skilled artisans working alongside him who developed the scientific instruments required for his work. Some of these instruments were already in use by European astronomers (albeit developed by Arab scientists) – astrolabes and armillary spheres, for instance (see plate 12) – but others were inventions of his own, such as the automatic mechanical clock that measured the true ascension of the stars and therefore gave the exact timings required for the five-times-daily Islamic call to prayer.

From his observations Taqi al-Din created new trigonometric tables with decimal points and functions including sine, cosine, tangent and cotangent – a new method for calculating solar parameters. His methods and instruments were evidently more accurate than those of Copernicus and Tycho Brahe, since he calculated the magnitude of the annual movement of the sun's apogee as 63 seconds, compared to Copernicus's 24 seconds and Tycho Brahe's 45 seconds.[2] Its true value today is known to be 61 seconds.

Another advance invented by Taqi al-Din in 1551 is a steam-rotated spit that turned wheels at the end of an axle, an important breakthrough in the development of the steam turbine. He wrote an explanation of the device in his work *The Sublime Methods of Spiritual Machines*, a title that gives a clue as to how he considered such inventions. He also described four machines for raising water, one of which is a six-cylinder pump with vertical pistons that predates many more modern engines, such as the rag-and-chain pump designed by the German scholar Georgius Agricola and described in his *De re metallica*, published in 1556.

The education system

The foundation of Ottoman learning and scientific advancement was first and foremost their education system, which was based initially around the institution of the *medrese* (Arabic *madrasa*, 'place of learning') inherited from the Seljuks and which developed further into the *külliye* system (see pp. 31–33).[3] Schools were often incorporated into the many buildings surrounding the courtyards of mosques, together with libraries, baths, soup kitchens, residences and hospitals for the benefit of the public. Under Süleyman the Magnificent, such schools, which were funded by religious foundations, provided a largely free education to Muslim boys. In Istanbul he increased the number of *mektebs* (primary schools), which taught boys to read and write as well as the principles of Islam; in addition, the *mektebs* often provided free meals and clothing. Writing as late as 1904, the British traveller Lucy Mary Jane Garnett wrote: 'There is perhaps no country in Europe in which primary education was provided for at so early a date as in Turkey, or so many inducements held out to poor parents to allow their children to participate in its benefits.'[4] *Mektebs* were co-educational: women were by no means excluded from education, though they could not progress into higher educational establishments.

Young men wishing to further their education could proceed to a *medrese*, whose studies included grammar, metaphysics, philosophy, astronomy and astrology; there were also higher *medreses*, which provided education at university level. *Medreses* were historically funded by the sultans. Each provincial town had at least one, and Istanbul is recorded as having over a hundred in 1904. Graduates of the *medreses* went on to serve in government and religious affairs as an educated class; while in theory the institutions were open to non-Muslims, in practice each religious community or *millet* tended to prefer to send its children to its own schools, run by teachers of their own religion and controlled by their own communities.

Like many scholars, Taqi al-Din had begun by studying theology before progressing into the field of science. Education was always at the core of the Ottoman system of government, and facilities were provided enabling the top scientists of the day to collaborate under the aegis of the court – partly, of course, because their work enabled the sultan to promote an image of power: his own and that of his empire.

Cartography

The Ottomans are not generally remembered for their prowess at sea, yet the Ottoman navy and its fleet played a powerful role in achieving maritime supremacy across the Mediterranean and beyond. In fact, it was on account on the Ottomans' domination of Eastern Mediterranean ports and cargo arriving via the Silk Road trade routes that the Spanish and Portuguese began their 'voyages of discovery', heading westwards, to America, and south, round the Cape of Good Hope, in search of other routes to India and China. The Ottomans had inherited a small fleet from their Seljuk predecessors, whose naval headquarters and arsenal can still be seen at Alanya, on the southern coast of Turkey.

At its height, the Ottoman fleet sailed as far afield as the Indian Ocean, sending an expedition to Indonesia in 1565. A whole century earlier, Mehmet II had conquered Constantinople by dragging his ships on greased planks up and over an entire hillside, to land them suddenly in the Golden Horn, a technical feat of immense ingenuity. It is rarely remembered, yet should easily rank on a par with Hannibal's much more lauded crossing of the Alps with his elephants, only one of which survived.

The most famous Ottoman admiral was Piri Reis ('Captain Piri': *reis* is Arabic/Ottoman Turkish for 'leader' or 'captain'). He owes his renown to his skills as a cartographer, as displayed in his *Book of Navigation*, in which he published one of the oldest maps of America still in existence. Drawn in 1513, just thirteen years after the earliest-known world map, it is remarkably accurate for its time.[5] It was discovered only in 1929, by a German theologian undertaking cataloguing work in the Topkapı Palace library. Before that, Turkish maps were given little attention or wrongly considered to be Italian, yet Ottoman nautical science was ahead of its time. When Piri Reis presented his new world map to Selim the Resolute in 1517, the sultan acquired an accurate description of the Americas and the circumnavigation of Africa well before many European rulers. The map bears an inscription by Piri Reis explaining how the map was composed:

> No one has ever possessed such a map. This poor man constructed it with his own hands, using twenty regional maps and some world maps, the latter including ... one Arab map of India, four maps recently made by the Portuguese that show Sind [modern Pakistan], India and China drawn by means of mathematical projection, as well as a map of the Western Parts drawn by Columbus ... The coasts and islands [of the New World] on this map are taken from Columbus's map.

No trace of any maps made by Columbus have ever been found, making this reference highly significant. If one were known, one big difference would have been immediately apparent: Islamic maps and European maps are drawn differently, and each would have seemed upside down when compared with the other (see plate 2). Muslims drew maps with the south at the top, not the north. European maps originally showed the east at the top, hence our word 'orientation'. Jerusalem, in medieval maps, was usually placed at the top or in the centre, because the Holy Land was considered to be the centre of the world.

Captain Piri's book also contained information detailing precise routes to the Mediterranean ports, how to approach them and where to take refuge in the event of a storm. A revised 434-page edition, prepared as a gift for Süleyman the Magnificent, contained 290 maps. Piri took part in many Ottoman naval wars against Spain and the republics of Genoa and Venice, including both battles of Lepanto in 1499 and 1500, where the Ottomans suffered their first ever defeat at the hands of the Europeans. He also participated in the 1516–17 conquest of Egypt and the successful siege of Rhodes against the Knights of St John, which led to the Crusaders' surrender and final departure in 1523. He died in Cairo in 1553, aged 88, executed for insubordination.

One of the most remarkable maps of the world ever made, full of such fine detail that it resembles a modern-day map, is the work of the 16th-century Ottoman Ali Macar Reis. It was produced as a collection of seven maps in 1567 but is today known as the Ali Macar Reis Atlas, covering the Black Sea, the Eastern Mediterranean, Italy, the Iberian Peninsula, the British Isles, the Atlantic coast of Europe, the Aegean Sea, western Anatolia and Greece.

Aviation

In the Ottoman explorer Evliya Çelebi's ten-volume *Seyahatname* (Books of Travels), there is a brief description of what has subsequently been dubbed 'the first intercontinental flight' by the Ottoman polymath Hezarfen Ahmed Çelebi (1609–1640),[6] who was said to have flown across the Bosphorus – in other words, from Europe to Asia.

First, he practised by flying over the pulpit of Okmeydanı
eight or nine times with eagle wings, using the force
of the wind. Then, as Sultan Murad Khan was watching
from the Sinan Pasha mansion at Sarayburnu, he flew from
the very top of the Galata Tower and landed in the Doğancılar
Square in Üsküdar, with the help of the south-west wind.
Then Murad Khan granted him a sack of golden coins,
and said: 'This is a scary man. He is capable of doing anything
he wishes. It is not right to keep such people,' and thus sent
him to Algeria on exile. He died there.[7]

Such is Ahmed Çelebi's popularity in Turkey today that one
of Istanbul's four airports is named after him, as is a mosque
next to the main Atatürk International Airport. His flight
has also been dramatized twice: in the 1966 film *Beneath My
Wings*, and the 2015–16 Turkish television series *Magnificent
Century: Kösem*.

Evliya also tells us that, in 1633, Ahmed Çelebi's engineer brother, Lagari Hasan Çelebi, launched himself in a
seven-winged rocket from Sarayburnu, below the Topkapı
Palace, using the equivalent of 38.5 kg (140 lb) of gunpowder.
The flight was supposedly to mark the birth of Sultan Murad IV's
daughter; Evliya Çelebi recounts how the engineer declared
to the sultan beforehand: 'O my sultan! Be blessed, I am going to
talk to Jesus!' After ascending in the rocket, he landed in the sea,
then apparently swam ashore and joked, 'O my sultan! Jesus
sends his regards to you!' Murad rewarded him with a gift of
silver and a knighthood in the Ottoman army.[8]

The 'robotic Turk'

One novel Ottoman legacy was the so-called 'robotic Turk'.
Originally called the 'Iron Muslim', then renamed the 'Ottoman

Turk', it was a machine dressed in a turban and Ottoman robes that appeared to play chess. It had a black beard and grey eyes, and its left arm held a long, smoking pipe. In 1770, at a time when mechanical devices were all the rage, the Hungarian inventor Wolfgang von Kempelen gave his queen, the chess-playing fanatic Empress Maria Theresa, the 'robot', which played chess skilfully and beat the best players of the time. It was immensely popular and functioned for eighty-five years, touring both Europe and America. It was, however, an elaborate hoax, because hidden inside the mechanism was a chess master who operated the model but never took the credit. Among the distinguished opponents who lost to it were Napoleon Bonaparte and Benjamin Franklin. Fifteen chess masters are recorded as inhabiting the machine over the course of its eventful lifetime, until it was destroyed by an unfortunate fire in 1854.

Military advances

The Ottomans had adopted gunpowder artillery by the 14th century, well in advance of their European and Middle Eastern adversaries. Before that, the earliest Ottoman fighting forces had relied on semi-nomadic Turkmen horsemen taking their enemies by surprise in shock raids at high speed, using weapons such as bows, spears, swords and daggers. Under Orhan (r. 1323/24–62), the son of Osman, the army – consisting mainly of foreign mercenaries not required to convert to Islam – had been paid a salary. Then, in 1389, a system of military conscription was introduced whereby every town, village or city quarter was duty bound to provide a fully equipped conscript. Called *azabs*, they were used to dig roads, build bridges and transport supplies to the frontline. Often recruited from among the homeless, criminals and vagrants, they developed a reputation for undisciplined brutality. One notorious branch of *azabs* was known as the *bashi-bazouks* (Turkish for 'crazy-heads'); drawn mainly from among Albanians, Circassians or slaves from Europe and Africa, they practised unbridled looting and targeted defenceless civilians. *Bashi-bazouk* as a colloquialism has come to mean 'undisciplined bandit' in many languages. In Hergé's *Adventures of Tintin* books, Captain Haddock often uses it as an insult, shouted at his enemies.

The janissaries (from the Turkish *yeniçeri*, meaning 'new soldier') began as a corps of infantry bodyguards armed with just bows and arrows, but by the time of Mehmet the Conqueror they had been drilled in the use of muskets and firearms, making them the first standing infantry force equipped with firepower in the world. In the 15th and 16th centuries this group constituted the most disciplined and feared military body of its time, mainly owing to its high level of organization, logistical capabilities and its elite troops. They were originally made up of young Christian boys taken in the *devşirme* from the western Balkans, but by 1570 Muslims were also accepted, and by the 17th century the janissaries were made up almost entirely of soldiers who were born Muslim, many of them from Albania.

Their command of logistics throughout the 15th and 16th centuries is what set the janissaries apart from other armies of the time: support corps prepared the roads, pitched tents for the camps in advance and even baked the bread on the road. Weapons were transported separately, and ammunition was resupplied by a specially trained support corps. Medical teams of Muslim and Jewish surgeons were taken on campaign, and the injured were treated in special mobile units set up behind the lines. In peacetime, the janissaries served as policemen, palace guards and firefighters. Yet by the mid-1700s what had been a highly efficient, elite military corps, greatly feared by adversaries, started to lose its grip on discipline: the janissaries became protectionist, enrolling their own children so that they too could benefit from good salaries and pensions, and also taking up other trades.

At the 1453 siege of Constantinople, a number of cannon were employed; they were mainly designed by Turkish engineers, but one crucial piece was the work of the Hungarian engineer Orban, who had first offered his services to the Byzantines, but at a price so high that Emperor Constantine XI could not afford it. Mehmet accepted his offer and was able to break down the previously invincible walls of Constantinople in just fifty-four days of relentless battering with the new cannon. A decade later, a Turkish engineer designed the so-called 'Dardanelles Gun' cast in bronze. It was still in use over three centuries later, and was employed against the British Royal Navy during the Anglo-Turkish War (1807–9).

The musket, a large, hand-held gun made of heavy steel that fired bullets capable of penetrating heavy armour, was also in use by 1465, giving the janissaries a big advantage over their adversaries. The Europeans and even the Chinese acknowledged the superiority of Turkish muskets by the 16th century, which were the first to use a rack-and-pinion mechanism. (Over the following centuries, the weapon gradually evolved into the lighter, easier-to-use rifle.) The janissaries were also the first to use volley-firing and the kneeling position for firing, at the Battle of Mohács in Hungary in 1526. During the confrontation, which was led by Süleyman the Magnificent, the janissaries had 2,000 muskets and fired them consecutively from nine rows, one after the other, so that one could reload while the other fired, to great effect. The Chinese later copied the Ottoman kneeling position for firing.

In the naval arena, the Ottomans designed the *Mahmudiye*, a warship that was for many years the largest in the world, boasting 128 guns over three decks. Constructed in 1829 at the imperial naval arsenal on the Golden Horn, it took part in many important naval battles, including the siege of Sebastopol (capital of the Crimea) against the Russians in 1854–55. Several warships and submarines in the modern Turkish navy are named after Piri Reis.

Mining

One extraordinarily pragmatic innovation by the Ottoman state that took place in the 19th-century context of accelerating industrialization was its method of extracting coal from the mines around Zonguldak on the Black Sea coast. In lush, green, heavily forested mountains that fell sheer to the coast – very difficult to access except by sea – were rich seams of coal scattered over the terrain. These were worked by about a hundred mines from the 1860s till 1920. The usual pattern during industrialization elsewhere in the world was for capitalist entrepreneurs to exploit the mines, as happened in the United Kingdom and the United States. The impetus for mining was the state's need for coal to power its steam-powered naval fleet and its steam-powered factories. To help fulfil this need, they put in place a regulation, by law, that the forty or so villages in the vicinity of the mines had to work the mines for a period of fifteen days every month, after which they were free to return to their villages for the remainder. They were paid fair wages for their labour and exempted from military service. It was an unusually imaginative scheme, based on the state's recognition that, realistically, the villagers constituted the only local labour force in that inaccessible area. The solution was far more humane than the terrible conditions in which coal miners were forced to work in Britain. As a result, the villagers evolved a unique social system in which they were not full-time labourers, exploited like factory workers in industrialized societies in the West, but neither were they full-time villagers.

Skilled technicians were brought in from other Ottoman provinces where mining already took place, such as Montenegro and Croatia, to provide expertise; they worked full-time in the mining process and earned good wages. Clearly, during periods when the young men were absent from their villages, the women were more involved in doing men's work than would have been the case elsewhere. They had to work in the fields and conduct the harvest as well as bring up the children. As a working model, it was unique, although the system gradually collapsed after the imported labourers went on strike for higher wages – something the local villagers never did. When they wanted to stop work, they simply put down their tools and walked home. This was their pattern, for example, on religious holidays, when they wanted to return home to celebrate with their families.[9] Today, the mines are no longer in use; the village streets are clean, and the beaches that were once black with coal dust have reverted to normality.

6
Literary Curiosities

OTTOMAN TURKISH is the only language in the world that has ever approached English in its richness of vocabulary, and for similar reasons. English incorporated countless elements not only from Latin and ancient Greek, but also from languages spoken within the British Empire and beyond. The Ottoman Turks, for their part, 'had at their disposal the entire learned vocabularies of the Persians and the Arabs, together with words from the speech of their Byzantine predecessors in Anatolia and of the sultans' European subjects'.[1] This supplemented and enriched their ancestral Turkish vocabulary, which itself already contained many other borrowings, from languages including Mongolian and Sogdian, amassed over the centuries.

In the Arab provinces, the use of Ottoman Turkish military terminology persisted in Syria, Egypt and Iraq even after Ottoman rule had ended, along with words relating to trade, such as *gümrük*, the Turkish for 'customs house'. In the Balkans, despite the fact that large numbers of Ottoman terms have been deliberately expunged from official languages, many are still widely used in both colloquial and literary languages throughout the region. They have become so much a part of Balkan culture that many non-Turkish speakers do not even realize that they are Ottoman in origin. For example, in Romania there are commonly used words such as *cizmă* ('boot', Turkish *çizme*), *masă* ('table', Turkish *masă*) and *chimir* ('belt', Turkish *kemer*). In Serbo-Croat, the word for 'bag' is *torba*, the same as Turkish *torba*, and that for button is *dugme* (Turkish *düğme*). Modern Greek, too, in spite of the attempt to expunge them after Greece achieved independence in 1832, retains a number of Turkish words, including *tembelis* for 'lazy' (Turkish *tembel*), *tsopanis* for 'shepherd' (Turkish *çoban*), and culinary terms such as *dolmades* for 'stuffed vine leaves' (Turkish *dolma*) and *tzatziki* for the yogurt dip made with garlic, cucumber and mint (Turkish *cacık*). More generally, the Ottoman linguistic legacy in cuisine lives on across the world, even in fast food, through words such as *yoğurt*, *baklava*, *kebab*, *rahat lokum*, *köfte* and *pilav*.

Few young Turks today know how to read Ottoman Turkish in its old Arabic script, so many are cut off from their own literary heritage. Only dedicated professional scholars still fully understand the old literature, and today's Turkish students simply read it in modern paraphrase. At the time the change was made from the Arabic script to the Latin alphabet in 1928, the census showed that only 1.1 million people out of a population of 13.6 million were literate.[2] Atatürk's language reforms were the most comprehensive ever achieved by any nation, and included a systematic purging of all language elements deemed to be foreign, but even now, when all Arabic and Persian words are supposed to have been expunged, and only one 'pure' form of Turkish is said to be in use, it remains striking how many modern Turkish words – especially for abstract concepts such as 'revenge' *intiqam*, 'justice' *adaala*, 'honour' *sharaf*, 'patience' *sabr* and 'duty' *wazifa* – are still Arabic, often borrowed through Persian.

Early epic poetry

The Turkmen tribes, like many Near Eastern and Central Asian tribes, lack a written history. Early Ottoman literary tradition was entirely oral, and consisted mainly of songs eulogizing the heroes of the first migrations and marches. The oldest examples of written Turkish are 8th-century inscriptions found in Siberia and Mongolia, in which the words 'Oghuz' and 'Turks' appear to describe two separate communities, sometimes at war, sometimes in alliances in which the 'Turks' are dominant. Over time, the word 'Turks', as the more powerful partner, came to mean both sets of people, and between the mid-10th and early 13th centuries the word 'Oghuz' was slowly supplanted by 'Türkmen' (English 'Turkmen') among the Turks themselves.[3]

The oldest genre in Turkish is the heroic epic. There are several, such as the *Oghuzname* (Book of the Oghuz), but the best known is the *Book of Dede Korkut*, which was highly influential in early Ottoman literature. It is a collection of twelve anonymous stories set in the heroic age of the Oghuz Turks, who migrated westwards in the 9th and 10th centuries, from the Altai Mountains and Lake Baikal to the lands east of the Caspian Sea. In their new home they came under the influence of Islam, since these lands were controlled by the Abbasid Arab caliphs of Baghdad. The now-Islamicized Oghuz then moved westwards again, and formed the bulk of the forces led by the Seljuk dynasty, who conquered Iran and Iraq in the 11th century and Anatolia in the 11th and 12th centuries. The Ottoman dynasty that gradually took over Anatolia after the fall of the Seljuks, towards the end of the 13th century, also led an army that was predominantly Oghuz. The Oghuz depicted in the highly entertaining and humorous *Dede Korkut* adventures are mainly the heroic *beys* (tribal leaders), their wives and relations. *Dede* ('Grandfather') is a common title for holy men in Turkey, and Korkut himself is the wise Oghuz tribal elder and bard who plays the lute at gatherings. The wives are always 'white-faced', as befits their rank, since sun-tanned skin implied outdoor manual labour, but the ideal Oghuz woman was no sickly retiring creature. Lady Chichek ('Flower'), the bey's daughter, as well as being 'purer than the moon, lovelier than the sun',[4] was also an excellent horsewoman, archer and wrestler. The tribe's circular domed tents, similar to those still used by nomadic Turkmen today, are described in colourful detail: even the smoke-holes are 'golden'.

Puppet theatre

Sophisticated theatrical drama did not develop in the Islamic world till modern times, but various forms of puppet theatre were enjoyed during the Ottoman period. It was popular at royal courts and village squares alike, and took the form of a dialogue between two characters, Karagöz ('Black-Eye') and Hajivat ('Ivat the Pilgrim'), who appear in an endless variety of disguises. Karagöz is depicted as an illiterate simpleton from the countryside, while Hajivat is a more educated city-dweller. Both were said to have been based on real people who worked in Bursa, the first Ottoman capital, on the construction of a mosque for Orhan in the early 14th century. Popular legend had it that they used to entertain the other workers with their antics but were eventually beheaded for slowing down progress. After their execution, the story goes, they simply picked up their heads and walked away, which certainly shows an ability among the early Ottomans to laugh at themselves. Puppet theatre spread to most parts of the Ottoman Empire, and it is still especially popular today in Turkey, Greece, Bosnia and Herzegovina and Adjara (today's Georgia).

Hajivat usually opens the show, giving a short introduction to the problem at hand, then says to the audience:

> This is the performance of shadows. It is an enigma for men of knowledge. You, looking at it with the eye of the spectator, stand amazed by its brilliance and try to understand its meaning; if you cannot understand, they say to you – it is a mystery.[5]

Easy to transport and set up in any location, the shadow plays were especially popular in coffee-houses during the thirty nights of Ramadan, drawing crowds after a day of fasting (a role now largely performed by television dramas watched at home on the sofa). Up till the 19th century the plays were full of political satire and contained plenty of sexual obscenities, but, ironically, they began to face repression after the Tanzimat reforms were brought in from 1839 to 1876, in an attempt to modernize the Ottoman Empire's old-fashioned state apparatus.

Essays on statecraft and morality

The Ottomans inherited a great many cultural and literary traditions from their Turkic Seljuk forebears, who had been fortunate to have as their grand vizier the highly cultivated and learned Nizam al-Mulk ('Keeper of Order in the Kingdom' in Arabic), a Persian Sunni. To help his early Seljuk masters including Alp Arslan and Malikshah, Nizam al-Mulk wrote (in Persian) the remarkable *Book of Government* in the form of advice to governors; later Ottomans such as Sarı Mehmet Pasha, treasurer to Ahmet III (r. 1703–30), adopted the same approach, likewise writing (in Turkish) a fascinating treatise on statecraft. Sarı Mehmet aspired to become the grand vizier to the sultan but never succeeded – ironically because he was insufficiently adept at manipulation and outwitting his rivals.

After fifty years of service, he was disgraced and executed. Here is a fragment of what he wrote about bribery in around 1714:

> Bribery is the beginning and root of all illegality and tyranny, the source and fountain of every sort of disturbance and sedition, the most vast of evils, and greatest of calamities ... there is no more powerful engine of injustice and cruelty, for bribery destroys both faith and state ... To give office to the unfit because of bribery is a very great sin.[6]

The Ottomans were fond of essays on the subject of morality, and one 17th-century writer, called Haji Khalifa, wrote *The Balance of Truth*, which included a pair of essays on tobacco and on coffee, substances whose effects were controversial and that the Ottoman state periodically attempted to ban, to no avail. Here is his advice on the evils of tobacco:

> Occasional reprimands from the Throne to smokers have generally been disregarded, and smoking is at present practised all over the globe ... But an evil odour arises in the mouth of the heavy smoker, halitosis is as aloeswood and ambergris ... The conclusion must be to recommend abstention ... there is no question of interference with those who have the addiction ... As most Muslims are addicted to it, they have become inseparably attached to the practice, and will in no circumstances be deterred from it or abandon it.[7]

The modern Turkish state finally banned smoking in all public places in 2009.

Poetry by the dervishes

Ottoman literature is sometimes unfairly dismissed as derivative and unoriginal, with one early 20th-century writer commenting that 'every fourth word of Turkish is Arabic, every third idea Persian'.[8] Poetry has always been the dominant genre – in Arabic, Persian and Turkish literature – and Turkish poetry has long been intimately connected with song, especially the mystic poetry of the Sufi dervishes who accompanied the Ottomans on their early migrations west. Most poetry was in fact expressly written to be sung, using the poetic metres of Persian poetry. This is another reason why so many Persian and Arabic words were used: they worked best with these metre systems.

The 12th and 13th centuries were a period of great political upheaval: the Abbasid caliphate in Baghdad was crumbling, and the Mongol armies were ravaging the eastern Islamic world. The Seljuk capital of Konya was one of the few places considered safe from the Mongol onslaught, so scholars, theologians, artists and intellectuals from all over the region fled their native lands to seek refuge at the Seljuk court. Among them was a Sufi master originally from the town of Balkh (today in Afghanistan), whose son went on to become a household name even in the West: Rumi, sometimes referred to simply as Mevlana (literally 'Our Master').[9] He died in Konya in 1273, and would therefore have been known to and contemporary with the Turkmen tribes who often fought on behalf of the Seljuks. His tomb lies beneath the striking turquoise-green dome of the *tekke* where his son (d. 1312) founded the Sufi Mevlevi sect, now known as the 'whirling dervishes' (see plate 9). The centre of the order was always Konya, but the whirling dervish dancing ritual spread Rumi's poetry and music throughout the newly emerging Ottoman Empire; many smaller *tekkes* were founded all over the empire's territory, as far away as Egypt and Syria. In Jerusalem a mosque lamp made in Iznik for Süleyman's renovations of the Dome of the Rock is dedicated to Rumi: it is inscribed with a *hadith* (saying) of the Prophet Muhammad comparing the believer in a mosque to a fish in water, while the non-believer is likened to a bird in a cage.

The population of Konya was partly Greek-speaking, since it had long been home to a strong Christian community, and partly Turkish, but the language of the Seljuk court was Persian, used in literature and poetry (see plate 13). Rumi wrote in this, his native tongue, as well as in Greek and in Turkish on occasion. His work was never as popular with Arabic-speaking Sufis, however, since its Persian imagery translated less well into Arabic.

Tolerance of those from other religions was always central to the Mevlevi order, as this excerpt from his masterpiece, the *Divan-i-Kebir*, illustrates:

> *Come, whoever you may be,*
> *Even if you may be*
> *An infidel, a pagan, or a fire-worshipper,*
> *Come.*
> *Ours is not a brotherhood of despair.*
> *Even if you have broken*
> *Your vows of repentance a hundred*
> *Times, come.*[10]

This is essentially how the highly stylized formal language of Ottoman Turkish, as used in administrative and literary contexts, was born: in the writing of what came to be known as 'Divan literature', *divan* being the Ottoman Turkish word for the collected works of a poet.

Turkish folk poetry was closely connected to Turkish folk music in the same way that Ottoman Divan poetry was intimately bound up with Turkish classical music: both often served as lyrics. Sufism's enormous influence on Ottoman literature can also be seen in the works of the astonishingly long-lived

Yunus Emre (1238–1328), who overlapped with Rumi but outlived him by some fifty years. Inspired by Anatolian folk poetry and its oral tradition, Yunus Emre was one of the first known poets to have composed in the spoken Turkish of his day. Less widely known in the West than Rumi, he remains popular in countries from Azerbaijan to the Balkans, and his tomb is claimed by seven different locations. His subject matter was mainly human destiny and divine love. The word *aşık* (which means 'lover') was used for first-level members of the Bektashi order of Sufis. Humour was an important part of Bektashi culture and teaching, often with the student poking fun at conventional religious views. One example tells of an imam preaching about the evils of alcohol, who asks his pupils: 'If you put a pail of water and a pail of *rakı* [an aniseed-flavoured alcoholic drink] in front of a donkey, which one will he drink from?' A Bektashi in the congregation immediately answered: 'The water!' To which the imam responded: 'Indeed, and why is that?' The Bektashi replied: 'Because he is an ass.'

Poetry by the sultans

Almost every Ottoman sultan from 1400 onwards wrote poetry, so deeply engrained was it in the Ottoman make-up. Most sultans were highly educated and could read and write in several languages. Reciting a well-known poem, or even one's own, was always viewed as a mark of cultivation. In the 16th century especially, poetry was so popular that one poet, Zâtî, exclaimed: 'I've struck it rich! Every two or three days somebody's servant comes along and brings me either a few silver coins or a few of gold accompanied by some delicious food or some halvah, and a letter that says "write me such and such a kind of poem".'[11]

Perhaps one of the most surprising rulers to compose verse was the ninth Ottoman sultan, the grandson of Mehmet the Conqueror, known to the West as 'Selim the Grim' (1465–1520), though the real meaning of his Turkish epithet *Yavuz* to Turkish speakers was closer to 'the Resolute' – a title earned from the enormous expansion of Ottoman territory he achieved. In his short reign of just eight years (1512–20) he defeated the Persian Safavids at the epic Battle of Çaldıran, then conquered the Mamluks in Syria, Egypt and the Arabian Peninsula, including the Holy Cities of Mecca and Medina. From that point on, the he assumed the titles of 'Caliph' and 'Guardian of the Holy Cities' – the latter representing the first time the role had fallen to a Turk and not an Arab. We are told that Selim slept just four hours a day and that, when he was not fighting, he was reading and writing. Fiery-tempered and impatient of others, he had a reputation for executing viziers if they did not live up to expectations; a popular Ottoman curse was: 'May you be a vizier of Selim's!' His mother, a Christian born in Albania, was a huge influence on him, and he himself married a Christian from Georgia, with whom he had four daughters and one son. This was the son who would go on to become Süleyman the Magnificent.

Selim wrote verse in both Turkish and Persian, using the pseudonym 'Mahlas Selimi', and some of his poetry is still extant today, housed in the imperial archives at the Topkapı Palace Museum. In 2018 the London auctioneers Bonhams offered a single sheet from a late 16th-century manuscript copy of his poetry for sale, with a guide price of £3,000–£5,000.[12] A collection of Selim's poetry was also published in 1904 in Berlin, by order of Kaiser Wilhelm II. In 1515 Selim himself had issued a decree, on the advice of the highly conservative *ulema*, the

religious elite, who wanted to restrict learning to the few, impos-
ing the death penalty on anyone using a printing press to produce
books in Turkish or Arabic.

Here is a translated example of one his many *gazels* (Arabic
ghazal, love poetry), a rhyming poem similar to a sonnet:

> *From Istanbul's throne a mighty host to Iran guided I;*
> *Sunken deep in blood of shame I made the Golden Heads to lie.*
> *Glad the Slave, my resolution, lord of Egypt's realm became:*
> *Thus I raised my royal banner e'en as the Nine Heavens high.*
> *From the kingdom fair of Iraq to Hijaz these tidings sped,*
> *When I played the harp of Heavenly Aid at feast of victory.*
> *Through my sabre Transoxania drowned was in a sea of blood;*
> *Emptied I of kohl of Isfahan the adversary's eye.*
> *Flowed adown a River Amu from each foeman's every hair –*
> *Rolled the sweat of terror's fever – if I happed him to espy.*
> *Bishop-mated was the King of India by my Queenly troops,*
> *When I played the Chess of empire on the Board of sov'reignty.*
> *O Selimi, in thy name was struck the coinage of the world,*
> *When in crucible of Love Divine, like gold, that melted I.*[13]

Süleyman the Magnificent and his *tughra*

Every Ottoman sultan from Orhan (1284–1359) onwards had
his own personalized *tughra* – a signature in the form of a cal-
ligraphic monogram that was used on all official documents
like a seal. It has been compared to the pharaohs' cartouches in
ancient Egypt and the royal cypher of British monarchs. It was
specially designed for each sultan by the court calligrapher but
certain elements are common to all, such as the loops to the left,
thought to symbolize the two seas under the sultan's dominion:
the larger one the Mediterranean, and the smaller, inner one the
Black Sea. The lines to the right are believed to signify a sword,

symbol of power and might, while the vertical lines possibly signify a flagstaff or, symbolically, independence; the 's'-shaped lines hint at winds blowing from east to west, the Ottoman's traditional direction of movement.

Süleyman's *tughra* was, fittingly, the most magnificent ever achieved. It was devised for him at the start of his reign, in 1520, and bears the words 'Süleyman, son of Selim Khan, ever victorious'. Below his name was written in exquisite Arabic-script Turkish calligraphy: 'This is the noble and exalted sign of the Sultan's name, the revered monogram that gives light to the world. May this instruction, with the help of the Lord and the protection of the Eternal, be given force and effect. The Sultan orders that...'.

The *tughra* appeared as a badge of authority, the stamp of the empire's power, at the top of all important official documents. Contemporary with Henry VIII of England and the Holy Roman Emperor Charles V, Süleyman is estimated to have issued about 150,000 such documents during his reign,[14] promulgating new laws, establishing diplomatic ties and creating a vast civil service to administer his empire.

Calligraphers were themselves important bureaucrats within the Ottoman government, and the reason they developed such a beautiful and densely packed intricate script was to prevent forgery through the insertion of extra words into the sultan's instructions. It must have been effective, given the survival of the Ottoman state right through till the First World War.

Süleyman's poetry

The tenth and longest-reigning of the Ottoman sultans – under whom the Ottoman Empire reached its apogee, comprising between 15 million and 25 million people across Europe, Africa and Asia, and whose fleet dominated the seas from the Mediterranean to the Red Sea and the Persian Gulf – Süleyman somehow also found time to write copious quantities of love poetry to Roxelana, his favourite concubine and, later, his wife, by whom he had six children. On top of all that, he instituted major legislative changes and reforms to society, education, taxation and criminal law, earning his Turkish epithet 'Kanuni', 'the Lawmaker'. He harmonized religious law, *shari'a*, with sultanic law, *kanun* (from the Arabic word *qanun* for 'law' and originally a Greek loan word, also source of the English legal 'canon'). He collected all the judgments that had been issued by the nine sultans who preceded him, eliminated duplications and contradictions, then issued a single legal code that would enable the rapidly changing empire to create a firm legal foundation. This code, called the 'Ottoman Laws', would last more than 300 years. In addition to his military, administrative and poetic skills, Süleyman was a great patron of the arts, literature and architecture. Today many consider his reign to be the golden age of Ottoman culture.

Süleyman and Roxelana's relationship lasted thirty-seven years till her death, but Süleyman spent ten of them away, on twelve different military campaigns, personally leading attacks against the Christian strongholds of Belgrade, Rhodes and most of Hungary before his conquests were halted at the first siege of Vienna in 1529. It is evident that he missed her greatly and, as she developed her political acumen, she became his eyes and ears in the capital during his absences. Ottoman poetry was always permeated by love and desire. Often it concerned the yearning of the Sufi dervish for union with God, or the idealization of male friendship, but also the passion of great romances. Here is one of Süleyman's love poems to Roxelana, entitled 'Throne of my

Lonely Niche'. It was possibly written while he was away during his campaign against the Persian Safavids, and was composed under his pen name Muhibbi (meaning 'lover'):

My solitude, my everything, my beloved,
My gleaming moon,
My companion, my intimate, my all, lord of beauties,
    my sultan
My life's essence and span, my sip from
The river of Paradise, my Eden
My springtime, my bright joy, my secret,
My idol, my laughing rose
I sing your praises, I wish you well
My heart filled with grief, my eyes with tears,
I am your lover [Muhibbi],
You bring me joy [Hürrem].[15]

Süleyman's most famous verse is:

The people think of wealth and power as the greatest fate,
But in this world a spell of health is the best state.
What men call sovereignty is worldly strife and constant war;
Worship of God is the highest throne,
    the happiest of all estates.[16]

Roxelana and her writing

In Western history and folklore, Roxelana (known principally by the Ottomans as 'Hürrem Haseki Sultan') is remembered as a scheming harlot, a seductress, even a witch, but the sources for these images are all reports by Europeans, often the ambassadorial dispatches of the Venetian and Genoese representatives in Istanbul. She is specifically blamed for instigating the murder of Mustafa, aged 40. (Six years older than her own eldest son, Mehmet, Mustafa was Süleyman's son by a different mother, an earlier concubine.) Mustafa had been very popular with the janissaries and had been widely expected to succeed Süleyman.

The Ottomans believed that every son born to the sultan (unless they were physically or mentally disabled) – by any of his concubines, all of whom from the early 14th century onwards were selected from Christian countries in the empire – had the right of succession. They did not practise primogeniture like the European dynasties. They believed natural competition between the sons allowed for the best candidate to prove himself and thereby created stronger rulers – a system that proved itself true to a large degree. It confined the conflict of succession to the family: it was often fratricidal behind closed doors, but was thought to spare the populace at large from such devastating civil struggles as the English Wars of the Roses. (The year of Roxelana's marriage to Süleyman, 1536, was the same year that Henry VIII had his second wife, Anne Boleyn, executed.) Roxelana's greatest legacy was the transformation of the royal harem into a political force, and under her tutelage it had become a regularized institution in the Ottoman government by the end of the century.

The young Roxelana had been trafficked as a slave girl from Ruthenia ('Little Russia', then ruled by the Polish king; today it mostly lies within Ukraine). It seems to have been Süleyman's mother, Hafsa Hatun – whose job it was to look for future talent and to identify the most beautiful, most healthy and most lively-minded women as breeding stock for her son – who spotted her potential as a future concubine. Such women were then converted to Islam and assimilated into Ottoman culture, learning Ottoman Turkish, Arabic and Persian. When they first met, Süleyman was 26, and she was just 17. Born a Christian to unknown parents (some believe she was the daughter of an Orthodox priest), Roxelana – which just means 'maiden from Ruthenia' – was renamed 'Hürrem' when she came to the Ottoman court, a Persian term that means 'joyful' or 'laughing'. To this was added the epithet 'Haseki', meaning 'the Favourite', once she had secured the attention of the sultan to the exclusion of all other concubines, even after bearing him the requisite son. When Süleyman married her in 1536, fifteen years into their relationship (and only, significantly, after the death of Süleyman's mother), she acquired the additional title of 'Sultan', and was addressed by everyone only by her title 'Haseki Sultan', as was the norm in Ottoman society; Süleyman would have been the only person who called her 'Hürrem'. No subsequent Ottoman sultan was to marry, and of the previous rulers Osman had been the only one to do so, for dynastic reasons, taking a Byzantine princess.

From the Ottoman side very little was written about Roxelana, since to write about women, especially married women – let alone those married to the ruler – was regarded as improper. The only other source we have for Roxelana's life and personality, therefore, is her own writing, some of which has survived. Turkish literary researchers have expressed great admiration for her mastery of the subtleties of Ottoman Turkish poetry,[17] especially since it was not her native language. Seven of her letters, written to Süleyman while he was away on his military campaigns or on prolonged hunting trips, are still in the Topkapı Palace library, written in lively and affectionate prose often lamenting his absence: 'If you ask after your wretched poor slave, day and night I burn in the fire of grief over separation from you.'

We can glean additional hints as to her character from the foundation deeds of the many religious complexes she endowed, both in Istanbul and across the empire, including in the holy cities of Mecca and Medina, and in Jerusalem. They show a caring side to her nature, as she gave special consideration to slaves, mindful perhaps of her own past, and was punctilious in setting down ways in which the staff of her foundations should treat the needy and sick with kindness and consideration.

While there had been an earlier tradition of Ottomans using the mothers or aunts of sultans as emissaries for important messages or even to negotiate peace treaties, Roxelana was the first woman of the Ottoman court to initiate diplomatic correspondence on her own account, writing letters to the king of Poland, Sigismund II Augustus, who ruled over the lands where she is thought to have been born. She began by offering the king her condolences on the death of his father and, after receiving a warm and welcoming reply, the correspondence developed a tone verging on intimacy, with a subsequent exchange of gifts to cement the friendship. Roxelana's daughter Mihrimah also wrote on her own behalf to further the friendship and alliance, and Poland remained one of Süleyman's staunchest allies. Roxelana's written exchanges were not limited to European rulers, for a few years later she also developed a cordial correspondence with the sister of the Persian Safavid shah, maintaining the peace and showing her diplomatic skills on the world stage, especially when she was acting as Süleyman's informant in the court while he was away. Roxelana also had her own *katibe*, a female scribe, rather like a private secretary – another first for a concubine.[18] Her initiative was followed by her successors, so that by the end of the century the mother of her grandson was corresponding with the Venetian government and with Catherine de' Medici, regent mother of the French king; and the subsequent queen mother corresponded with and exchanged gifts with Elizabeth I of England.

The phenomenal success of the Turkish television series *Magnificent Century* (sometimes dubbed 'Magnificent Controversy'), particularly popular in Bulgaria and the other Balkan countries, goes some way to correcting the Western image of Roxelana. When it first aired in 2011, the Turkish government media regulator received over 70,000 complaints from people offended at the loose morals and harem scenes it depicted. President Erdoğan himself agreed, calling it 'disrespectful' and saying it showed 'our history in a negative light to the younger generations'.[19] Screened in sixty countries round the world, including across the Middle East, in Italy and even in the United States, it also showed audiences how the six children Roxelana bore Süleyman in quick succession – five sons and one daughter – were central to her life. Every concubine who bore the sultan a son had a duty to raise her son for a future political role in the empire and to accompany him on that journey, which generally began with a prolonged posting as governor of a province, such as Amasya or Trabzon. Roxelena's course broke with tradition: instead of being dispatched after their first son was born, she stayed in the palace to bear the sultan a total of five sons.

Wine poetry

It may surprise many to learn that poetry written in praise of wine forms a whole genre in the Islamic world. The Qur'an tells us that wine tasting of musk and camphor is drunk in paradise, and the undisputed master of the genre was Abu Nawas

(756–c. 814), who wrote for the caliph of the Abbasid court in Baghdad. Wine poetry continued to be composed in the Arab world till the late Ottoman period, and the Ottomans, as Hanafi Muslims, believed that drinking weaker wine (*nabidh*, as opposed to *khamr*) was permitted. The following *ghazal* was written by Baki (1526–1600), considered the 'sultan of poets', the son of a humble muezzin who won the friendship of Süleyman the Magnificent, then Selim II, then Murad III. In translation so much is lost, but his poems, written in Turkish, were admired even beyond the empire during his lifetime for their technical skill and smoothness of expression. Wine could be said to have been the downfall of the empire: Süleyman's son and successor, Selim II – also known as 'Selim the Sot' – preferred to remain permanently drunk than face the administrative tedium of running an empire. He died by slipping on a marble bathhouse floor, in a state of inebriation. His rule marks the beginning of the Ottoman decline.

> *Now's the time, O vintner's lad, when wine lends flavour*
> > *to the cheer;*
> *Let us drink a glass or two – or even more – for spring is here!*
> *Scented breezes, crimson roses, all that's glorious in spring –*
> *God the Bountiful in such wise lets his graciousness appear.*
> *Let this moment slip not by; for in the garden of the world*
> *Happiness, no more than roses, cannot last an endless year.*
> *Now is not the time for praying nor for public pieties;*
> *Rather does the season call for fun and frolic loud and clear.*[20]

An Ottoman poetess

One exceptional woman poet was Mihri Hatun (1460–1506), who succeeded in holding her own in the early cultural centre of Amasya, a place much favoured by the Ottomans in the 15th and 16th centuries as a seat of learning. Future sultans were often sent there to learn about the different communities of the empire as part of their training, since every *millet* – Greek, Armenian, Jewish, etc. – was represented in the province.

Mihri Hatun is the only Ottoman woman poet whose work survives today, unique within the male-dominated sphere of early modern love poetry. Often called the 'Sappho of the Ottomans', she was from a prominent family, the highly educated daughter of a *kadi* (an Ottoman judge). Her privileged background meant that she benefited from strong patrons and never needed to marry. She did not take a male pseudonym but wrote openly as a woman, using complex gender images such as 'the menstrual fluid of men', talking explicitly of her desire for men, at a time when her male colleagues wrote only about idealized abstract love for God or for 'young boys', not for women. In one of her poems she writes: 'I came to the battlefield of love … My heart burns in flames of sorrow/Sparks and smoke rise, turning to the sky/Within me the heart has taken fire like a candle/My body, whirling, is a lighthouse illuminated by your image.'[21]

Evliya Çelebi, travel writer par excellence

Another writer who occupies a unique position in the field of Ottoman literature is the much-quoted Evliya Çelebi (1611–c. 1685), whose monumental ten-volume *Seyahatname* (Book of Travels) is one of the longest and most ambitious travel accounts by any writer in any language. A member of the Ottoman elite (his father was chief goldsmith to the sultan), pious and yet unconventional, Evliya was a cultured man whose vivid descriptions bring to life the colour and variety he saw all around him: his reflections convey a picture of what it was like to live under the Ottoman Empire. Obsessively curious about everything, he began travelling in his thirties, embarked on the Hajj to Mecca in his early sixties, and eventually died in Cairo in his seventies.

Osman of Timişoara, 'Prisoner of the Infidels'

Autobiography was extremely rare in Ottoman literature, but a vivid account of life as a Muslim prisoner under various Habsburg masters and mistresses was discovered languishing in the British Museum, then published for the first time in German in 1954. In it, Osman of Timişoara, captured during the chaos that followed the failed second siege of Vienna in 1683, describes the cruelties – and occasional kindnesses – he experiences during his twelve years in 'enemy' territory, before he finally succeeds in escaping back to Ottoman lands.[22]

Osman Hamdi Bey

Osman Hamdi Bey (1842–1910), intellectual, archaeologist and painter, studied nine years in Paris under French artists. He was the first to draft laws to counter the smuggling of artefacts out of the Ottoman Empire – a practice that Europeans had routinely carried out. He was the founder of the Istanbul Archaeological Museum in 1881.

The theft of Ottoman antiquities and artefacts was a popular theme in the British cinema of the 1960s, in the days before mass tourism, when far fewer people travelled beyond Europe to what were perceived as 'exotic' locations. The 1964 film *Topkapi* starred Peter Ustinov as a petty thief who gets inadvertently roped into helping steal the famous Topkapi Dagger, encrusted with the world's most prized emeralds. The gang of thieves is led by Melina Mercouri, erstwhile Greek culture minister, and also stars Maximilian Schell and Robert Morley. Shot on location, it depicts a cheerfully chaotic Istanbul, with some astonishing scenes, during daylight hours and after dark, of the thieves running round on the lead-domed roofs of the Topkapı Palace. Based on a book by Eric Ambler, *The Light of Day*, it won an Academy Award in 1965, while Peter Ustinov won Best Supporting Actor. It earned $7 million at the box office.

7
Musical Traditions

OTTOMAN COURT MUSIC (what is now known as Turkish classical music) was developed in the Ottoman court at Istanbul and in the *tekkes* (monasteries) of the dervishes. It was played by several instruments according to open-ended modal systems and was never written down. This absence of notation encouraged improvisation and allowed a certain freedom in performance. (Some scholars argue that, once music is written down, originality and inventiveness are inevitably stifled and forfeited.) The traveller Evliya Çelebi recorded that there were some forty guilds of musicians in Istanbul in the 1670s.

Like Arabic music, Ottoman Turkish music is based on a series of melody types called *makam* (from the Arabic *maqam*), introduced to the Ottomans by the Seljuks. They, in turn, had first encountered them in Baghdad, where polymath scholars including Al-Farabi (*c.* 872–950) invented the *rabab*, a stringed instrument like a kind of guitar. During the Islamic golden age Al-Farabi went on to write *The Great Book of Music*, along with five other works on music that were later translated into Hebrew and Latin. The American composer and musicologist Carl Engel noted that the 'Arabs, when they came to Europe, in the beginning of the 8th century (Muslim Spain), were more advanced in the cultivation of music [and] in the construction of musical instruments, than were European nations.[1] It is worth remembering that Arabic music in Andalusia went on to influence the development of flamenco in Spain, and of the fado tradition in Portugal.

The vowel harmony of the Turkish language gives it an innate musical quality, one reason it is sometimes called 'the Italian of the East'. Like poetry, music was passed down orally, with the *makam* system of melodic phrases, scales, aesthetic conventions and modulatory traditions also acting as a set of rules for improvisation. There were many local variations, but the tradition of *makam* was in place across the Arab world from Syria to North Africa, offering a huge richness and diversity. Most of this music is played on instruments resembling the fretless lute, where an equal division of notes into the Western-style octave does not apply. (Our word 'lute' comes from the Arabic *'oud*.) It features twenty-four divisions of the octave compared to the twelve equal semitones of the Western system, meaning that this type of music often sounds 'out of tune' to the Western ear.

Mystical Sufi music

The Seljuks brought Sufi dervishes with them when they entered Anatolia, a tradition continued under the early Ottomans. The Sufis recognized music as having sacred qualities, as a source of ecstasy, and as capable of bringing man closer to God. Konya and Sivas are the great centres where popular folkloric music can still be heard in religious gatherings across Anatolia: performers use the *saz* as a principal instrument, a kind of lute beloved of mystic poets.

Al-Farabi wrote about the philosophical principles of music, its therapeutic effects on the mentally ill and on the soul, and its cosmic qualities, all of which underlie the musical traditions of Sufism, thought to have been first developed in Baghdad. The deep-rooted spiritual aspect of Ottoman music has its origins in these mystical dervish traditions, using delicate and gentle-sounding wind and string instruments including the *kemençe* (a string instrument with a bow, played like a viola) and the *tanbur* lute, and especially the haunting *ney* (a reed flute) favoured by the whirling dervishes of Konya. It was learnt orally and passed from master to pupil, perfected through practice.

Music education at the Ottoman court

Ottoman classical music was nurtured at the Topkapı Palace, just as it had at the court at Edirne, the Ottoman capital before Istanbul. The Ottoman court enrolled young boys and girls to be educated, and anyone who showed musical ability would be trained. The teachers were often professionals on the Ottoman payroll and would have their own private students when they were not at the palace. Even the sons and daughters of the sultans were required to undergo musical training if they had the aptitude. Several of the sultans composed music, including Selim the Resolute. One of his best-known pieces, written just before a battle near Isfahan in 1514, was an exhortation to his troops to fight.

In addition to a general musical education, efforts were aimed at teaching particular instruments. These included the *'oud* (an early form of the lute), panpipes, the *zurna* (a relative of the oboe, made from fruitwood), the drum, the *saz* (similar to a guitar), the *kemençe* fiddle, and the zither (a plucked string instrument played on the lap). Musicians formed part of the entertainment put on for the benefit of the sultan and the harem members, either individually or in ensemble.

Women in the Ottoman musical tradition

The 500-year-old tradition of Ottoman music included the contributions of women as composers, performers and teachers, especially in urban centres. Some were able to receive a musical education, and were taught to sing and play instruments, while others were largely self-taught.

Documentation from the 16th century survives showing that musical ensembles in the palace during the reign of Süleyman the Magnificent included players of the *çeng*, an Ottoman harp that was always played by women (see plates 14 and 15). A French merchant of that time who accompanied the French ambassador on a visit to Istanbul and who then stayed for seventeen months observed that the Turks listened to music while eating, and that women played the harp, the *kemençe* fiddle, the *tanbur* lute and the *kanun* zither, and that some sang and danced with castanet-like *çalpara*. Other European commentators of the 17th century noted that young concubines in the palace played instruments, sang and danced, and that they were free to come and go from the palace as long as they informed the gatekeeper. Sometimes palace concubines took lessons from male musicians in the city, staying for weeks in the homes of their masters, and other times musicians came into the palace to give them lessons. The daughter of the palace doctor, Leyla Saz Hanim (1850–1936), who lived for many years in the palace, recorded that there was an all-female band and orchestra in the harem comprising sixty members. She wrote that the sultan's wife and daughters were all educated in the study of the Qur'an, Ottoman history, poetry, books and newspapers, and were also taught how to play instruments including the piano, the violin and the *lavta* (a kind of lute).

Western-style music started to enter the Ottoman cultural sphere only in the second half of the 18th century; we know, for example, that when a harpsichord was brought from Paris in the early 1700s, it did not meet with Ottoman approval because it could not reproduce the tones they were used to.

Military bands

The Ottomans were the first to maintain a permanent military band as part of their army, a tradition that started in 1299 when the Seljuk sultan is said to have presented Osman, the first Ottoman sultan, with a group of musicians to thank him for helping to fight their mutual enemies. The band would follow the sultan's army during expeditions and sometimes deliberately arrive, playing as loudly as possible, in the middle of battles to raise morale and to terrify the other side. Over time they became part of the janissaries, who maintained a band of six to nine members playing instruments such as drums, the *zurna* (oboe), clarinets, triangles, cymbals (*zil*) and kettle-drums of war (*kus* and *naqqara*), carried on the backs of camels. The performers were known collectively as *mehteran*, from the Persian meaning 'seniors'; the singular, *mehter*, was used both for the type of music itself and for an individual performer.

After they were defeated at the Battle of Vienna in 1683, the janissaries, retreating in haste, abandoned their musical instruments on the battlefield, enabling their enemies to learn from them and then start up their own European military bands. Napoleon Bonaparte's bands were equipped with Ottoman war instruments such as cymbals and kettledrums, and his victory at the Battle of Austerlitz (1805) was said to be due in part to the psychological effect his noisy bands had on the enemy.

An obsession with 'the exotic'

In Europe it became fashionable to present performances using Ottoman Turkish instruments, in the 'Turkish fashion', at ambassadorial receptions. By the 18th century the Western fascination, verging on obsession, with everything to do with the 'exotic' Orient and the Ottoman imperial harem was reflected in music including Mozart's *Turkish Rondo* and his opera *Die Entführung aus dem Serail* (The Abduction from the Seraglio). A young Rossini wrote *L'italiana in Algeri* (The Italian Girl in Algiers) and *Il Turco in Italia*, in which a daring gypsy woman who has escaped the harem and a handsome prince named Selim from Istanbul are characters depicting 'the other'; Prince Selim even offers to buy the wife of his rival, as if such behaviour were the norm for Turks. Such stereotypes fed deeply into Western perceptions.

From 1828 to 1856 Giuseppe Donizetti, the elder brother of the famous Italian opera composer Gaetano Donizetti, held a position at the Ottoman court as Instructor General of the Imperial Ottoman Music. He had previously served as band-leader in Napoleon's army during the campaigns against Austria and had been present at the Battle of Waterloo. Known as 'Donizetti Pasha', he taught music at the sultan's palace to members of the imperial family, even composing the first national anthem of the Ottoman Empire. Ladies of the harem learned to play the piano on instruments imported from Vienna, and the Ottoman military bands played marches that Rossini and the Donizetti brothers had written expressly for them. Such was the passion for the ballroom music of Europe in Istanbul at the time that members of the imperial family even began composing their own polkas, marches and waltzes. Franz Liszt was among the eminent musicians who visited Istanbul, and it is clear that there was considerable musical interchange between Europe and the Ottoman court during that era. Donizetti came to see Istanbul as his second home and, when he died there in 1856, he was buried in the vaults of the St Esprit Cathedral in Pera (today's Beyoğlu), the district where many foreign embassies and wealthy European merchants are based to this day, and where the Genoese-built Galata Tower is located.

Roxelana-inspired music

Roxelana, wife of Süleyman the Magnificent, has inspired a powerful body of work in both opera and ballet, her colourful life making for perfect entertainment. In her birthplace, she is proudly commemorated in concerts by the Ukrainian Symphony Orchestra[2] that feature such compositions as the 'Dance of the Three Girls' from the ballet *Hürrem Sultan*, by the Turkish composer Nevit Kodallı, and pieces from the ballet *Roxelana* by Dmytro Akimov. She also gave rise to the theme music from the television series *Roxelana* and the opening theme from the wildly popular Turkish costume drama *Magnificent Century: Roxelana*, both of which can be heard on the internet.

Links between Ottoman music and Greek church music

The Greek Orthodox population of the Ottoman Empire, including the Armenians and other ethnic groups, enjoyed a common musical culture.[3] Their musical cooperation and exchange resulted in a musical lingua franca. Even now, common characteristics are evident in the music of the Balkans and the Near East that were once under Ottoman rule. The music of the Greek Orthodox Church survived in a religious context and continued to develop in subsequent centuries. It was never stamped out or suppressed by the Ottomans. In fact, many have observed that the Serbian national identity can be said to have been preserved thanks to the autonomy the Serbian Orthodox Church enjoyed under the Ottoman *millet* system. From the 17th century onwards there was even a regeneration of so-called 'post-Byzantine' music, in which Ottoman music was seen as an important source of musical inspiration and technique, valued as an instrumental counterpart to purely vocal church music. The two music types share a close relationship, since both regarded the human voice as the most perfect musical instrument, with its ability to produce minute differences in pitch.

Cultural nationalization in the Balkans and Greece

There are several Ottoman-influenced urban music traditions in the Balkans that are easily detectable to this day. In Greece, for example a large part of the café repertoire recorded in the 1920s and 1930s consisted of popular Ottoman music that was given Greek lyrics and played by Greek musicians; and the same occurred in Macedonia and Bosnia. This Greek-language café music remained popular as far afield as Egypt and the United States well after the dissolution of the Ottoman Empire, where it was performed in cabarets, theatres, nightclubs and brothels.

The connections between Ottoman popular music and *smyrneika* (i.e. music from Smyrna, modern Izmir) are often unacknowledged these days. Smyrna is presented as a Greek city with a separate Greek music tradition, as is Thessalonica, described as the purely Greek capital of the purely Greek province of Macedonia. Yet both were multi-ethnic cities and, in 1917, before the great fire of Thessalonica, Greek-speaking Orthodox Christians were only the third-largest group, coming after the Sephardic Jews and the Muslims. Their music was clearly Ottoman-influenced.

Judging from photographs of well-known Ottoman Greek musicians playing Ottoman instruments, there is no doubt that such music was performed at cafés and taverns in Greece well into the 1930s. In the United States Greek musicians and their Turkish, Jewish and Armenian colleagues went on recording and performing the Ottoman repertoire even after the Second World War (see plate 16). A boom in modernized Ottoman and Turkish music in Greece began in the early 1960s, and a revival of Ottoman Greek café music in Greece began in the mid-1970s, when some remakes of old songs became major hits.

Despite this evidence, a traditional account of age-old Greek national culture as an unbroken lineage reaching back to Classical times is still reinforced in Greek school teaching, along with texts such as *The Hellenic Art of Music: 2,500 Years of Hellenic Music History*. In such books, Greek national music is presented as a symbol of the continuously perennial Greek nation, which, following the golden ages of Classical Greece and Byzantium, experienced a dark period under the Ottoman Empire but finally regenerated culturally, politically and territorially through heroic struggle.

The language issue

As we have seen, the various religious and ethnic groups of the Ottoman Empire represented a great linguistic diversity. Many Greek and Armenian Orthodox Christians spoke Turkish as their first language, and it was sometimes written using Greek and Armenian characters. There were also Turkish-speaking Slavs, Armenian-speaking Greeks, Greek-speaking Jews and Greek-speaking Levantine Catholics. The largest of these groups were the Turkish-speaking Christians of Asia Minor and Constantinople, who are mentioned in documents as early as the

15th century. This language situation is reflected in recordings by Ottoman Greek café singers that contain a mixture of languages, usually Greek and Turkish. At one time there were also LP records with one side sung in Greek and the other in Turkish. *Rebetiko*, the Greek term referring to a type of urban song style popular from the late 1800s, originated in the coffee shops of towns like Smyrna and Thessalonica.

In 2017 *rebetiko* was added to UNESCO's Intangible Cultural Heritage list. The use of Greek in song justifies the inclusion of an Ottoman piece in the Greek national repertoire. Tracing the Ottoman origin of Ottoman Greek pieces is often difficult for the modern scholar since the Ottoman Turkish popular repertoire is itself in large measure forgotten.[4] The so-called *chaabi* music (from the Arabic *sha'abi*, meaning 'of the people', 'folk'), still popular in Algeria today, was also heavily influenced by Ottoman culture and played on stringed instruments such as lutes.

8
Medical Mores

IT MAY SURPRISE MANY to learn, given that so many Western Europeans associate the Ottoman Empire with violence and military aggression, that the Ottoman approach to caring for the sick, both physically and mentally, was often more enlightened than in Europe. Physicians tended to begin from a holistic standpoint, seeking to create the best ambience in which the body and mind could heal themselves, treating patients gently and with kindness (see plate 17). The importance of music therapy was understood: it was based on the sound of running water, combined with the soothing effect of aesthetically pleasing surroundings in the form of beautiful architecture and gardens. The properties of certain food and drinks were also investigated. Caring for the sick in the hospitals was a practice instituted by the Ottomans' predecessors, the Seljuks, who were the first to found such establishments, known variously as *darüşsifa*, *darüssıhha* and *şifahane*, all of which mean 'place of healing'. They were funded through the religious *waqf* system, based on charity and open to all social classes. Injured Crusaders are even recorded as preferring Muslim doctors because of their superior knowledge.

Ottoman surgeons

The Ottomans invented several surgical instruments, some of which are still in use today, including the forceps, scalpel, pincers, lancets, and the catheter.

One of the most notable Ottoman surgeons and physicians was Şerafeddin Sabuncuoğlu (1385–1468), who lived to the age of 83, despite trying out many cures and remedies on himself before applying them to his patients. At the age of 80, he completed his illustrated medical textbook *Cerrahiyyetü'l-Haniyye* (Imperial Surgery), which he presented to Mehmet the Conqueror. It was written in rhyming verse, as was normal in teaching materials at the time, since it made it easier for students to remember. Strikingly, women appear as surgeons in the illustrations; referred to as *tabiba* (Arabic for 'female doctor'), they played key roles in the field of gynaecology.

Among Şerafeddin Sabuncuoğlu's innovations was a method for helping both mother and child in childbirth, including a speedier delivery of babies: the woman held her breath and pushed to exert a stronger downward force. He even recommended herbal drugs that caused sneezing, thus causing more downward pressure to push the baby out. He described a process to drain fluid from the skull in children suffering from a condition that is now known as hydrocephalus; it was not officially classified until 150 years later, by Marco Aurelio Severino, an Italian surgeon who died of the plague in Naples in 1656. Sabuncuoğlu described the dangers of bacteria, pathogens and sepsis, and wore surgical garments and a mask to prevent their spread, as well as using wine and olive oil as antiseptics. His book even describes the surgical removal of small cancers from the breast to prevent them spreading. He was based at Amasya in central Anatolia, an early Ottoman centre for commerce, culture, learning and the arts, where he ran the hospital for fourteen years. Today the beautiful 14th-century building, known as the Darüşşifa ('house of healing'), built round a courtyard with a fountain that provides the soothing sound of running water, is used for concerts and other public events while also serving as the Sabuncuoğlu History of Medicine Museum. The rooms surrounding the courtyard feature displays of 18th-century surgical equipment and explanations of historical medical procedures.

Dervish healers

Contemporary with Sabuncuoğlu was another Ottoman medical scholar, Akşemseddin, known primarily for his religious poetry and still revered today as a mystic saint. Born in Damascus in 1389, he served as tutor and adviser to Mehmet the Conqueror, founded the influential Shamsiyya-Bayramiyya Sufi order, and continued the early Ottoman tradition in which dervishes lived alongside sultans. He had previously studied as a dervish pupil under Haji Bayram Veli, from whom he is said to have acquired his medical knowledge.[1] Dervishes were traditionally experienced in healing not just physical diseases, but also psychological and spiritual illnesses. The early Turkmen tribes often had a 'healer', who would generally be a dervish, and even a 'healing tent', where the sick or wounded were taken to be cured. Instead of being locked up and abused, as they were in Western European countries, patients with mental illness in the Islamic world were helped using the calming influences of music, water and nature. Diet was also known to be important, and patients were fed a simple vegetarian diet and given soothing herbal teas to drink. At the end of their stay in hospital, they were given money with which to buy clothes and food before being released into the outside world, in recognition of the fact that they would not be able to go straight back into paid employment. Mental hospitals of this kind were geared to the total rehabilitation of patients in the community, and the aim was that there should be no repeat admissions. Many such hospitals were in use right up until the beginning of the 20th century, such as the Bimaristan Arghoun in Aleppo. Travelling through the Habsburg borderlands, Evliya Çelebi observed:

> Strange to say, by God's wisdom, there are not as many
> madmen in the German lands as there are in Turkey
> and Arabia. Still, there are many famous infidels in these
> asylums, and no one can find a cure for them.[2]

Like Sabuncuoğlu, Akşemseddin noted through observation how diseases spread, and wrote a work called *Maddatul-Hayat* (The Material of Life), in which he described microbe theory some 200 years ahead of Antonie van Leeuwenhoek (1632–1723), the Dutch scientist known today as 'the Father of Microbiology': 'It is incorrect to assume that diseases appear one by one in humans. Disease infects by spreading from one person to another. This infection occurs through seeds that are so small they cannot be seen but are alive.'[3]

Public health and hygiene

The promotion of public health and hygiene was a responsibility the Ottoman state took seriously. It ensured the availability of clean running water at public fountains, free for anyone to use. The Ottoman bathing culture also encouraged cleanliness through regular 'deep cleans' of the skin, and Istanbul was said to have boasted some 1,400 public toilets at the empire's height, at a time when such things were still a rarity in European cities and many Christian Europeans believed it was purer not to bathe at all. Soon after the 1453 conquest, ad hoc cleaning operations were instituted, and by the early 16th century street cleaners were employed to collect rubbish and dispose of it centrally.

The Ottomans developed policies in the realm of disaster prevention and health management as early as the 16th century. There are accounts of travellers having to quarantine outside the city for seven days if they were arriving from places suspected of having the plague. New regulations were introduced mandating the burial of plague victims outside the city walls, and records of daily death tolls were kept. Extra help and services were provided for the funeral industry, and the state offered tax relief to individuals and communities affected by the plague.[4] Businesses such as tanneries and slaughterhouses were moved outside the city as they were believed to contaminate the air.

On Ottomans and pandemics

Plague was a persistent problem throughout Ottoman history, from the Black Death in the mid-14th century right up to the dissolution of the empire in 1922. Epidemics broke out at regular intervals, on average every ten years or so in the empire's early centuries. Later, plague outbreaks were sometimes so frequent that they happened almost every year, leading the Ottoman state to make a number of institutional, legal and medical interventions from the early 16th century onwards. 'Ottoman society became familiar with outbreaks of plague over time, and in a way learned how to live with it,' notes Nükhet Varlık, a historian of early modern medicine: 'The response to plague was one of the elements that made the Ottoman state what it became during the sixteenth century: a state that monitored, controlled and managed the health of its population.'[5]

Varlık's studies have shown that public health administration was fully in place in the Ottoman Empire in the 16th century, well in advance of public health systems in Western societies. The empire was able to offset the loss of life that resulted from major outbreaks by expanding its territories in the 16th century and attracting immigrant populations to make up for labour shortages. But by the 17th century additional problems such as drought, famine, war, banditry and mass migration made it far harder for the state to recover.

By the 18th century special buildings called *tahaffuzhane* (from the Arabic *tahaffuz*, meaning 'precaution') were built as quarantine stations at various points along the Dardanelles, where ships and their crew were kept in isolation for many days before being allowed to continue into Istanbul.

The Black Death and the rise of the Ottomans

Some scholars have made a convincing case that the Black Death played a role in facilitating the rise of the Ottomans.[6] Arriving in Constantinople from the Crimea in 1347, it had originated in the Central Asian steppes, an area that was – and some would say still is – a natural reservoir for plague. It is thought to have spread with the Mongol invasions of the 13th century into Burma and Yunnan, where it became endemic in rodent populations. It erupted in China for the first time in 1331, and then made cyclical appearances throughout the 14th century during the rebellions and civil war that culminated in the collapse of the Mongol Yuan dynasty and the rise of the Ming dynasty (1368–1644).

From Constantinople it spread into the Balkans, then to Italy by sea, reaching Sicily, Marseille and Alexandria in 1347, as well as Cairo, Tunis and Damascus in 1348 through Mediterranean trade routes. From Damascus it spread north into Anatolia and east to Baghdad by 1349. By 1351 it had subsided in the Middle East, the last outbreak being in Yemen. In Europe the final manifestation was in Russia in 1353.

The Black Death was extremely destructive for the Byzantine state, eliminating a significant proportion of the population of the capital, Constantinople – partly because it occurred after two civil wars during the 1320s and 1340s that left it weakened, stripped of cash and vulnerable to Venetian, Genoese and Ottoman opportunism. Suffering a manpower shortage and facing threats from Serbia and Bulgaria, as well as civil war, the Byzantine emperor John VI Kantakouzenos concluded a pact with Süleyman, son of Orhan. He invited the Ottoman Turkish armies to cross the Dardanelles, thereby giving them a presence in Rumelia. The Ottomans took advantage of this situation two years later, when an earthquake destroyed many Byzantine strongholds and allowed them to capture the fortress of Gallipoli and move deeper into Byzantine territory. From that point on, the Ottomans became major rivals of the Byzantines. Most of their conquests of strategic significance took place after the Black Death. After Gallipoli in 1354, they took Edirne in 1365, which became their new capital. Thrace and Macedonia were conquered in the 1370s and 1380s. Extensive parts of the Balkans, including Sofia, were taken in 1382, Albania in 1385, Thessalonica in 1387, and most of Serbia by 1389.

More natural disasters afflicted Byzantine cities over the following years, so that by 1453, when Mehmet the Conqueror took Constantinople, the city's population had dwindled to barely 30,000, with only a few thousand soldiers left to defend it.

Constantly on the move, the Ottomans, as a nomadic people, were far less affected by the Black Death than the sedentary, urbanized Byzantines. The rodents that carried the plague thrived in densely populated areas, often spreading from the coast via ships that docked at port to conduct trade with inland cities. It therefore also ravaged the Turkic *beyliks* along the Aegean and Mediterranean coasts, playing a role in their eventual incorporation into the Ottoman state.

Historians have estimated that, in the period from 1346 to 1353, between one-third and two-thirds of Europe's population was killed by the plague. The recurrence of plague, wars and famines prevented Europe's population from recovering before the early 17th century. For example, in Normandy in the 1420s the population was only about one-quarter of what it had been on the eve of the Black Death, and similar patterns were observed in England. Mortality rates in Egypt and Syria were thought to be similar: Ibn Khaldun (1332–1406), known as the 'Father of Sociology', reported congestion in cities owing to the vast number of funeral processions taking place, while whole villages were deserted. The resulting labour shortages meant there were not enough people to work the land and maintain the irrigation systems, leading to big declines in agricultural yield. The cost of living went up, rents rose, and there was an exodus from the countryside to urban centres.

The education of Ottoman women in medicine
The first properly trained female Turkish physician, Safiye Ali, studied medicine in Germany before opening her own practice in Istanbul in 1921, the year before the Ottoman Empire fell.

Centuries before receiving a formal training in medicine, women were recognized as skilled 'healers' in Ottoman society with great experience in certain areas, especially childbirth and gynaecological practices. Documents in the Topkapı Palace archives show that the head physician to the sultan in the mid-17th century summoned a famous female physician from Scutari to heal three female patients. One woman doctor who succeeded in curing Abdulmejid, the heir to the throne in the early 19th century, was thereafter given a monthly salary and free entrance to the harem. Some were also employed at the quarantine office for post-mortem studies, according to a document dated 1842. Another woman physician is commemorated in the form of a verse engraved on her 1802 tombstone in the cemetery at the Kücük Ayasofya ('little Hagia Sophia'): 'Alas! The female physician, her own ailment she failed to heal.'

Skills were passed down from mother to daughter, and female physicians were also recorded as preparing drugs for treating syphilis, stomach swelling, eczema and diarrhoea in children. Female healers of alopecia were often documented as being Jewish, whereas women who treated phobias are described as 'pressers on the fear vessel' (believed to be located somewhere in the intestines).

Female nurses were employed at the palace school and the harem hospitals, where the head nurse was known as the 'Baş Hatun'. Formal education for nursing as an independent profession began at the start of the 20th century and continued with the treatment of wounded soldiers during the Balkan Wars (1912–13) and the First World War. Florence Nightingale had practised nursing during the Crimean War (1854–56) at the Selimiye Barracks in Üsküdar, Istanbul – a huge building that was allocated to the British as a temporary military hospital – and served as a model for both the British and the Ottomans. Today the northernmost tower of the barracks houses the Florence Nightingale Museum.

The remainder of the Selimiye Barracks is used today as the headquarters of the First Army of the Turkish Land Forces. Originally built of wood by Selim III in 1800 as part of the Ottoman military reform efforts, the barracks were burnt down six years later during a revolt of the janissaries but rebuilt in stone in 1825 on the orders of Mahmud II.

The practice of vaccination

Another area in which women were the chief practitioners was vaccination, whereby a small dose of a disease-causing organism is given to a person to stimulate the immune system into producing antibodies to fight that disease. It was widespread in the Ottoman Empire long before the English physician Edward Jenner was credited with pioneering the technique. The Anatolian Turks had inherited the practice from earlier Turkic tribes and called it *ashi*, or 'engrafting'. They had discovered that if they 'engrafted' their children with cowpox, taken from the udders of cattle, they became immune from the disfiguring and often fatal disease of smallpox. A postal stamp issued by the Turkish Postal Authority in 1967 commemorated the 250th anniversary of the first smallpox vaccination in 1717 and shows a child being inoculated by a woman inside a Turkish bath, flanked by a surgeon's scalpel and a sharp-nibbed instrument (see plate 18).

Today smallpox has been all but eradicated thanks to vaccination programmes, but it used to kill around 10 per cent of the population, or as much as 20 per cent in towns and cities, where infection spread more easily. It is perhaps apt that the revolutionary BioNTech/Pfizer vaccine for COVID-19 was developed by a Turkish couple living and working in Germany.

When the technique of vaccination was first brought to England from Ottoman Istanbul over 300 years ago, it was initially rejected. There was fierce opposition both from Church authorities, who opposed any form of intervention, and from most physicians of the time. Such was the suspicion with which it was viewed that the first trials were performed on condemned prisoners, who were promised their freedom if they survived – which they did. Rather than Jenner, it should be Lady Mary Wortley Montagu (1689–1762) who took the credit for introducing the concept of vaccination. Herself disfigured by an earlier bout of smallpox, and having lost her brother to the disease, she was living in Istanbul as the wife of the English ambassador to the Ottoman court in 1716–18 and came across vaccination being practised, quite probably in a Turkish bath. Keen to spare her own 6-year-old son, Edward, from the disease, she arranged for him to be vaccinated in spring 1718 by an 'old woman', under the supervision of the embassy doctor, Charles Maitland. She subsequently sent letters, published posthumously, back to friends in England describing the process in detail.

> I am going to tell you a thing that I am sure will make you wish yourself here. The small-pox, so fatal, and so general amongst us, is here entirely harmless by the invention of ingrafting, which is the term they give it. There is a set of old women who make it their business to perform the operation every autumn ... The old woman comes with a nut-shell full of the matter of the best sort of smallpox, and asks what veins you please to have opened ... She immediately rips open that you offer her with a large needle ... and puts into the vein as much

venom as can lie upon the head of her needle ... Every year
thousands undergo this operation ... There is no example
of any one that has died in it; and you may believe I am well
satisfied of the safety of the experiment ... I am patriot enough
to take pains to bring this useful invention into fashion in
England; and I should not fail to write to some of our doctors
very particularly about it, if I knew any one of them that
I thought had virtue enough to destroy such a considerable
branch of their revenue for the good of mankind.[7]

Upon returning to England Lady Montagu continued to spread
the Turkish tradition with great tenacity, having Maitland inoc-
ulate her own daughter in 1721 under the observation of the
Royal College of Physicians, whose president (and the founder
of the British Museum), Hans Sloane, was also present and
later gave it his endorsement. As a result, many of her relations agreed to be vaccinated. Word spread ever wider, and the
breakthrough came when a scientific description of the vaccination process was submitted to the Royal Society in 1724
by Dr Emanuel Timonius, who had been the Montagu's family
doctor in Istanbul. As a result, inoculation was adopted in both
England and France, nearly half a century before Edward Jenner
(1749–1823), a doctor from Gloucestershire, 'heard' that cowpox provided immunity from smallpox in 1796. Following the
successful experiments on prisoners, the children of Britain's
royal and upper classes were the first to be vaccinated, before it
became available to the general population.

Sultan Abdulmejid I (r. 1839–61) issued a royal mandate in 1840
by declaring that vaccinations should be provided to everyone,
free of cost. Children who were unvaccinated were expressly
prohibited from attending school, while their vaccinated
counterparts were presented with official certificates giving

their names and the vaccinator's name. Vaccination was also obligatory for state workers, students at schools and military personnel. Any staff who accepted students without certification would be fined. By 1903 the regulation was extended to include all workers in factories, businesses, shops and hotels, both men and women, and also migrants – an especially important factor at a time when the empire was experiencing increasing waves of internal and international migration on account of displacements caused by socio-economic and political factors. In 1915, as the Ottoman Empire entered the First World War, it issued a law prohibiting any citizen from wilfully evading vaccination, and declared that 'every person in the Ottoman Empire must be vaccinated three times by the age of 19' (at 6 months, at 7 years old and at 19 years old).

In practice, the empire never realized its goals since this would have required impossible resources, both financial and in terms of manpower. The ruling Young Turks (1908–18), the group who effectively overthrew the sultanate, made matters worse by purging the minority communities who had provided significant numbers of doctors and other trained medical personnel. The Turkish Republic inherited the public health institutions and staff that remained, but it was also heavily burdened by the empire's many unfinished projects and by heavy wartime debts.

Animal welfare

One of the first animal hospitals in the world was established by the Ottomans in the 19th century, the 'Helpless Stork Foundation' in Bursa. At a time when basic human rights were being discussed in Europe, the Ottomans had established a hospital for migratory birds, treating broken wings. Elaborate birdhouses designed to look like miniature mansions were built on the exterior walls of caravanserais, mosques and palaces, while birdbaths were placed on gravestones, symbols of the value placed on birdlife. Such acts of charity by citizens were seen as good deeds and encouraged, especially in urban settings, with care of street animals such as cats and dogs regarded as a religious duty.

The *New York Times* has estimated that, in Istanbul alone, there are currently thought to be around 130,000 dogs and 125,000 cats roaming free.[8] The Ottoman love of animals lives on in a Turkish law guaranteeing the protection of stray animals from cruelty. The ensuing bond between stray dogs and the people of Istanbul is beautifully documented in the 2021 film *Stray*.

9
Aesthetic Sensitivities

O you painters who ask for a technique of colour –
study carpets and there you will find all knowledge.
PAUL GAUGUIN

CARPETS OFFER A UNIQUE window into the prevailing aesthetic across the six centuries of Ottoman rule, unconsciously charting its trajectory from nomadic tribalism to urban sophistication. From the striking geometric designs of bold tribal nomadic rugs, the preferred style began to reflect a settled urban taste once silk workshops had been founded in Bursa. Heavily influenced by both Chinese and Persian floral designs, commissions from the Ottoman court in Istanbul cemented the trend towards luxury from the 15th century onwards.

Scholars today usually consider the art of carpet-weaving to have originated with the Turkic people and not with the Persians, as is generally assumed in the West. Persian carpets are more familiar to us, having reached Europe earlier and in greater numbers, with the result that researchers have historically neglected the study of Turkmen rugs in favour of Persian ones. Yet it was the Turks who invented the symmetrical hard-wearing double knot, known as the 'Turkish knot' or the 'Gördes knot' – much stronger and tougher than the Persian asymmetrical 'towel-technique' weave, which is only wrapped round a single warp.

Turkish carpets first appeared in France during the time of Louis IX (r. 1226–70), sometimes called St Louis – the only canonized French king, whose reign is remembered as a medieval golden age when the kingdom reached an economic and political peak. He had been exposed to Middle Eastern culture and tastes while living in the Latin Kingdoms of the East for four years following his capture in the ill-fated Seventh Crusade (1250–54). Owing to their artistic designs and vivid colours, these carpets were much coveted in Europe as high-status possessions, used to decorate walls and tables since they were considered too precious to serve as floor coverings. Venetian and Genoese merchants bought them from market places in Anatolia and shipped them into European cities. With their growing awareness of the Ottoman Orient, many Renaissance painters began to feature Turkish carpets in their paintings as objects of luxury, sophistication and prestige. Since there are more such paintings than there are rugs from this period, these images – by such artists as Carpaccio, Bellini, Holbein, Lotto, Vermeer and Van Eyck – together form a valuable body of reference, allowing scholars to confirm that tribal weaving followed age-old patterns across the centuries. Many paintings by Holbein (*c.* 1497–1543) feature rugs as a background (see plate 19), such as the famous portrait of Henry VIII, legs astride.

As European influences peaked, the carpets took on a Baroque flavour. The decline of the Ottoman Empire in the 19th century was reflected in its carpet production: the pressures of mass commercialization resulted in inferior quality and design. Since the 1980s, however, there has been a revival of traditional methods thanks to organizations such as DOBAG,[1] the German-Turkish Natural Dye Research and Development Project, whose efforts have fortuitously coincided with the nostalgic neo-Ottoman revival of recent decades. Common to all periods, however, is the astonishing Ottoman sense of colour harmony and the successful juxtaposition of bold shades, quite unlike European combinations. This is what Gauguin sensed in carpets: their powerful mystic symbolism and vigour. European art, he felt, had become too imitative, too artificial and stale. This same intense colour sense and design is what also makes Iznik tiles instantly distinguishable from Persian or Armenian tiles.

Carpets and tribal identity

To understand the Ottoman aesthetic, therefore, it is essential to grasp what a central role carpet-weaving played in the nomadic Turkish (or more correctly, Turkmen) identity. Carpets were the only tent furniture, their bright colours turning these movable tribal homes into versions of paradise, their warmth keeping the bitter cold of the steppe at bay. The carpet evolved out of this history, an expression of the Turkmen desire for a better, more beautiful life in the face of perpetual struggles to attain secure pastures for their flocks. (The Turkmens were frequently forced by advancing Mongol armies to migrate from their native Central Asian lands.) Their entire livelihood rested on the health of their sheep, sold at local markets in order to survive. Rug-weaving was collective work and relied on skills passed down through the generations. Families and tribes pooled their knowledge, skills and expertise.

In such a landscape, ringed with hostility, these rugs displayed an incredible wealth of ornamental variety. Such well-balanced colour schemes and harmonious compositions are a testimony to the magnitude of the Turkmens' achievement, accomplished in the face of continual adversity, constant competition over pastureland for their livestock, the menace of disease, and perpetual conflict, not just with rival tribes, but also with the forces of nature in the form of drought, flood, and extremes of heat and cold.

Here, then, is the essence of the Ottoman aesthetic: something you use in your everyday life must also be a thing of beauty. It is reminiscent of William Morris's motto centuries later, which acted as a template for the 19th-century Arts and Crafts Movement: 'Have nothing in your house that you do not know to be useful or believe to be beautiful'. It worth noting in this context that adherents to the Arts and Crafts Movement tended to assume that all 'Eastern' inspiration derived from 'Persian' – rather than Arab, let alone Turkish – design.

The oldest-known carpet-making centre in history is Konya, the Seljuk capital in central Anatolia. Marco Polo lauded the Konya carpets as the finest in the world and mentioned the existence of workshops under the patronage of the Seljuk sultans in the 13th century. A few rare pieces from this period are still exhibited in carpet museums in Istanbul and Konya. It was the Seljuks who spread the art of weaving across the Islamic world.

The materials used in the production of carpets reflected what was available, namely wool from the empire's vast flocks of sheep. The value of the carpets was judged according to the quality of the wool and the brightness of the colours, the highest quality of wool coming from sheep sheared just once a year, in the spring, and ideally taken from the shoulders, flanks and thighs of an adult sheep. Where possible, the sheep were driven into streams or rivers to wash them before shearing. That was men's work, but sorting the wool into various qualities before it was combed and spun was undertaken by women. Spinning is a slow and time-consuming process, and one person is able to spin just 1 kg (just over 2 lb) of thread per day.

Next came the dying process, another task performed collectively by the women. The skills required in collecting the relevant plants and insects, then making the correct proportions of dye bath to fix the colours, were crucial in determining the quality of the finished article. The spun yarn was first soaked in huge cauldrons in a weak solution of alum, copper sulphate, ferrous sulphate, tin or urine to ensure that the dye would fix to the fibres. After an hour or so it was transferred to the dye bath and soaked till the desired colour had been achieved. Lastly, the newly dyed yarn was washed and rinsed thoroughly to remove dirt and excess dye before being hung up to dry in the hot sun.

Red comes from the local madder plant, which can produce varying shades according to the age of the madder root, the hardness of the water and the additives in the dye bath. The strongest and deepest reds come from crushed beetles, while all shades of blue are produced from the indigo plant, which is dissolved in an alkaline solution. Green is produced from walnuts and olive leaves, while brown can be the result of natural undyed wool or derived from dried walnut pods or acorn cups. Yellow can be produced from over twenty plants, including saffron, wild chamomile, buckthorn and the pomegranate tree. These natural dyes are much more resistant to fading than the synthetic dyes first introduced in the 19th century, even in extreme sunlight. Reds and blues predominate, as does the *gül*, a stylized repeated medallion pattern thought to have developed as a tribal symbol or heraldic crest from animal designs with totemic significance dating back thousands of years. It was how the tribe proclaimed its identity – its essential 'passport' in illiterate societies.

Carpet design and symbolism

The themes of these carpets, when examined closely, are always the same: primeval patterns and colours that represent water, fertility and warmth. They could even be said to reflect the archetypal dreams of the women, yearning for an everelusive peace and security.

Each tribe used specific motifs (*göls*) that were symbols of its independence yet also significant unifying factors deriving from their common ancestry in the Turkic Oghuz tribes, with whom they shared their racial heritage, a common language and culture. From these shared elements sprang a common Turkmen concept of design. A tribe that lost its independence after being conquered by another took on the *göl* of the victors. A vanquished tribe thus lost its *göl*, though it might be permitted to use it on small items; in this way the *göl* was transformed into a *gül*, an ornament without tribal significance. The heraldic function also gradually lost its importance once a tribe became fully settled; carpet designs thus reflected changes in political and historical realities. The rugs are ringed with protective borders that resemble fences enclosing garden-like spaces full of flowers, trees and animals. Sometimes these borders have continuous rows of projections like spear points, and sometimes they have a successive line of birds' heads looking defensive, as if to ward off threatening forces or demonic influences. Although the preparation of the wool and the dyeing was a collective process, once the weaving on the loom began each rug was different, the product of an individual woman, reflecting her thoughts, fears and longings, in silent form through symbols.

Rug symbolism offers a window into a pre-Islamic heritage rich with myths and magic, portents and omens, where the use of symbols gave protection, prosperity, fertility and joy, in both

145

the material and the spiritual world. No one told the women what to weave – the images came out of their heads, informed by generations of mothers and grandmothers passing on their wisdom. Rugs were essentially made for domestic use only, but were also an insurance against hard times. Sale of precious dowry weavings – a family's most treasured possessions – would only be as a last resort.

Young girls were taught the art of weaving from around the age of 7, in order to prepare their dowry for their marriage at around the age of 15, when they would move into a new tent with their husband. The nomadic lifestyle has all but died out today in Anatolia, as has the ancient art of tribal weaving, but well into the 19th century a young Turkmen girl was expected to bring to the marriage tent a large carpet for the principal seating area opposite the main entrance, two small rugs, one rug for hanging inside the door, two decorated hanging panels for dividing the tent space into sleeping and living areas, twelve small bags for personal belongings such as jewelry, sewing kits and clothes that would be hung round the tent walls, and two large bedding bags for the matrimonial bed. Each bag had a specific function, for instance the storage of tent poles or animal trappings, cradle and sofa covers, or cooking pots and utensils.

The bride and groom would stand on one of the smaller wedding rugs to take their marriage vows. The door hanging, known as an *engsi*, symbolized the gateway to paradise, divided into the four symbolic gardens of paradise (as mentioned in the Qur'an), within which rises the cosmic tree connecting the underworld to heaven – a concept that helps explain Osman's dream about the overarching tree of his future empire. The tree's seasonal cycle follows the universal cycle of birth, maturity, death and rebirth, and it had a special importance for the Turkmen tribes. The tent dweller felt spiritually secure upon entering his or her tent through this *engsi* doorway.

Vases and ewers depicted on prayer rugs symbolize life-giving water and the waters of paradise. The symbols and patterns used in tribal rugs were never random. They held deep meanings for their weavers, putting them in harmony with the universe or providing magical protection. When this great tradition was alive, it was a form of communication, a language understood by everyone in the tribe and passed down from mother to daughter by word of mouth. As a result, when the commercial pressures of the 19th and 20th centuries bore down on tribal weavers, leading them to produce as many rugs as possible for the Western market in the shortest possible time, the ancient art of weaving and its design symbolism were forgotten, making it difficult for outsiders to recover the meanings.

Nevertheless, certain primeval, archetypal symbols are unmistakable, such as the sun as a disc and the moon as a crescent. The sun developed many stylized forms, such as a disc containing a cross to indicate its four points – east at dawn, overhead at midday, west at sunset and underneath at night – or a rotating solar cross that we recognize today as a swastika, which evolved into a symbol for subduing the power of evil by breaking it down into four parts. The metaphysical sun was the most important symbol, representing life, vitality, prosperity and everything good, which is why it was used so prolifically on tribal rugs. Often it was represented as a double-headed sunbird, possibly an eagle, which over the centuries became so stylized that it looked more like 'latch-hooks', as carpet dealers generally call them these days. Double-headed eagles as symbols of power we recognize today from the emblems of the Holy Roman

Empire, Russia and the Byzantine Empire, but the Seljuks also used them on gateways at their capital, Konya, as did the Hittites (*c.* 1650–1200 BCE) in their mountain fortresses in central Anatolia and the Assyrians all over the Near East and Mesopotamia. At Palmyra, the *cella* (holy of holies) of the Temple of Bel boasted a magnificent carved-stone ceiling centred on an eagle, now sadly destroyed.

Since the accumulated knowledge that informed the carpet designs was never written down, it is up to new generations of researchers, using their powers of deduction, to work out the messages contained in weavings and other tent furnishings. Few cultures apart from the West have produced conceptual frameworks and analyses for their own art, which makes conceptualizing the aesthetics of non-Western cultures, past or contemporary, problematic. Analysis and criticism are themselves products of the West – of classical and modern thought – with the result that everything has tended to be seen through a Western lens and interpreted through Western cultural limitations and historical contexts, however irrelevant these may be to the art itself.

Thankfully, Turkish academics are now at the forefront of this work, seeking to understand their artistic heritage without reference to the accepted norms of European art history. One of the most comprehensive explanations of Turkish carpet symbolism can be found in a museum in Gaziantep, in southeast Turkey, in a series of nine panels displayed in the upstairs rooms of a fine 400-year-old Ottoman whirling dervish lodge called the Mevlevihane Vakıf Müzesi. The juxtaposition of carpet symbols and Sufi mysticism in a shared space reveals how closely the two are connected in the Turkish mind. As well as illustrating the myriad symbols used in the carpets to convey messages about eternity and family, life and death, birth and reproduction, love and unification, the museum perfectly evokes the essence of Mevlevi philosophy, open to everyone.

Flowers and masculinity, geometry and nature

Once an attempt is made to understand how formative these early tribal origins were, the importance in Ottoman art of nature, especially gardens and flowers, becomes clearer. In no other culture are men so regularly depicted wearing or smelling flowers. Even today, Turkish men of all ages can be seen walking round the streets of cities and villages, wearing flowers behind their ears or tucked into their clothing.

All this is at odds with the Ottomans' reputation for military might and violence. The aesthetic of Iznik tiles also reflects this paradox, embodying two almost contradictory elements: there is a disciplined geometry and symmetry within each tile, but also an extreme sensitivity to nature and its manifestations. At an Istanbul-based online course examining Ottoman tile design in 2021, I was fascinated to learn just how structured the underlying designs are, even while they exude a strong sense of free-flowing vegetation. The common three-ball pattern known as *çintimani*, for example, represents a stylized version of animal-skin patterns, based on leopard spots and tiger stripes. The motif represents the same dual identity – the fierceness of wild animals softened into natural symbols that resemble leaves and flowers, such the *saz* leaf, hinting at a wild mythical forest.

Underlying the styles and patterns in Iznik tiles that are so recognizably Ottoman, it is tempting to see a steely strength and firmness, a toughness and resolve that may be lacking in Persian equivalents, with their softer and more effeminate qualities. It is a distinction that also reveals itself in the contrast between the harsher, stronger sounds of the Turkish language – words such as *yok*, the ultimate negative – and the gentler, more sinuous modulations of Persian. Persian-speakers themselves acknowledge a difference, as revealed by their own proverb: 'Flatter in Arabic, reprove in Turkish, but argue in Persian.'

Blend this underlying toughness, which can only be a deep-rooted relic of their harsh nomadic lifestyles and maybe even of their earlier shamanistic belief system, with the new spiritual sensitivities acquired when they adopted Islam from their Seljuk forbears and you begin to grasp the essential Ottoman Turkish aesthetic, so distinctive. What Islam brought to the equation, and which complemented Ottoman firmness so well, was its underlying mathematical rigour and discipline, its fundamental geometry, which, once your eye is trained to see it, enhances the natural rhythms hidden in every Iznik tile, just as they are hidden within nature itself. This quote, from the 10th-century Sufi philosophers known as the 'Brethren of Purity', shows that the power of geometry had long been understood:

> Know, o brother ... that the study of sensible geometry leads
> to skill in all the practical arts, while the study of intelligible
> geometry leads to skill in the intellectual arts because this
> science is one of the gates through which we move to the
> knowledge of the essence of the soul, and that is the root
> of all knowledge.[2]

Integral mysteries

Islamic art is built upon these mysteries and upon the fact that, as with God, there is no one starting point: infinity stretches endlessly in all directions. It is a concept that Western art, with its need for hierarchy and fixed points in a recognizable order, has difficulty comprehending. Once this essential difference in the perception of space is acknowledged, our appreciation of Islamic art and architecture will be much enhanced. Western art criticism has often dismissed Islamic art as being simply decorative, through a failure to appreciate its underlying geometric rigour and spiritual quality. Ornamentation is integral to the structure, not an afterthought. Carpets and kilims are decorated while they are being made, and the decorative motif is contained within the carpet's structure, like a mosaic floor.[3]

Through their perfect harmony of pattern and colour, repeating endlessly, the effect of these patterns on an open-minded viewer is to induce a state of spiritual calm, enabling them to feel closer to God by allowing themselves to be drawn inwards into a meditative state. In Arabic this concept is known as *fana'*, which translates in mystical Sufi Islam as something like 'extinction of the ego' or 'obliteration of the self'. The same term is used by whirling dervishes to describe the aim of the sema dance, in which, as the pace increases, the dancer aims to find God.

Turkish ceramics, in the same way as Turkish carpets, were intended to be used on a daily basis, not kept for special occasions. Magnificent Iznik tiles were produced as decorative elements in the architecture of mosques, while bowls and dishes bearing similar designs and colours were used every day at the Topkapı Palace and in the homes of wealthy Ottomans. They were not considered to be objects of art in the way they were in Western countries, where they can be found in large numbers in museum collections. The word for wall tile in Turkish is *çini*, derived from the word for 'Chinese', and the blend of earlier cultures on which the Ottomans built, especially in the case of ceramics, needs to be acknowledged.

Craftsmen

Artisans and craftsmen were mobile, both through choice and, at times, under compulsion. As one specialist in Islamic art has noted, 'Craftsmen with their special skills had value, and were one of the more useful spoils of war. This was particularly true of potters.'[4] It is a well-documented fact that the Mongols abducted craftsmen during their invasions in the 13th (under Genghis Khan and his sons) and early 15th centuries (under Tamerlane) to work for their new rulers. Many Persian tile craftsmen were taken from cities such as Tabriz, in the north-west corner of modern Iran, which was much fought over as an important commercial and cultural centre. It was the capital of the Karakoyunlu (Black Sheep) Turkmens, who, like the Ottomans and the Seljuks, were descended from the Central Asian Oghuz tribe. Their tiles appear in Damascus, Edirne and Bursa, where at least one of the tiles in the Green Mosque (Yeşil Camı) is inscribed: 'Made by the masters of Tabriz.' Excavations show that Iznik had a ceramic-producing tradition before the Turks captured it in 1331, but the Ottomans' techniques represented a complete break with Byzantine traditions, employing technology that had its roots in the Islamic world. From this point on the surviving Seljuk tiles and ceramics from Anatolia, Iran and Mesopotamia show a new momentum, with the appearance of fresh styles and techniques. Konya in Turkey, Kashan in Persia and Raqqa in Syria became the new leading centres for tile and ceramic production.

Artistic overlaps

It is important to recognize how all forms of artistic creation were connected in the Ottoman mind. Not only were the same motifs carried over from carpets to textiles to tiles, for example, but they were also repeated in dishes and plates.

Where ceramics feature human figures, they echo those in Turkish miniature paintings, where in turn they bring to mind the Turfan wall paintings of the Uighur Turks of Central Asia and conform to a conception of manly beauty found in Islamic art: a large, round face, almond-shaped eyes, small mouth, full cheeks, thin nose and long hair. Figures are depicted in a naturalistic style, mounted on horses or sitting cross-legged – a position known as 'Turkish sitting', borrowed from Asia during the early stages of Islamic art and thought to imply 'a good life'. Some figures have halos round their heads, indicating noble birth. They are often shown holding a handkerchief, fruit, a flower or a cup. Architecture is depicted in an enigmatic way in the miniatures, with inside and outside interchangeable – as, indeed, they often can be in Ottoman architecture, where a tent can become an echo of the landscape.

Sinan, the great 16th-century court architect, carried these artistic connections even further in his writings, where he sees architecture as a kind of spatial poetry – an interesting crossover that is reminiscent of Goethe's statement, centuries later, that architecture was frozen music. As the following passage illustrates, Sinan himself focused on the visual aesthetic of a building rather than structural issues, observing the ways in which it imitated the beauties of nature:

> The domes of the mosque were like waves that decorate the top of the open sea. The large domes resembled a picture that was drawn on the sky in gold ... Its coloured and decorated glasses changed colour in every light, like the wings of the Archangel, and offered every moment the beauty of spring gardens. These glasses that were adorned with the colours of the rainbow left everyone in admiration like the colours of the chameleon which change with the rays of the sun.[5]

Sinan conceived each space as a circular unified whole, filled with light and devoid of the hierarchy that typified Christian architecture. His aim was for the worshipper to feel closer to God, freed from the mediating clergy who were given such prominence, with special seating at the front, in the linear architecture of churches. His intention was to create an atmosphere of pure happiness: 'The pleasing interior halls of the mosque were like recreation places that increased one's joy.'[6]

In the midst of this cross-fertilization, the Ottoman fixation with carpets remained a constant. Sinan is known to have commissioned ten large, top-quality carpets for the Süleymaniye Mosque. The *qadi* (judge) of Küre was asked to oversee the production of these carpets 'day and night', and to make sure that they exactly followed the design samples and specified size and pattern type. The foundation deeds of several mosques confirm this ongoing fixation, listing the type of carpets endowed by their founders.[7]

Calligraphy

The aesthetics of Ottoman calligraphy evolved across the centuries of rule, with early examples favouring the use of diverse scripts, as can be seen in the walls and dome of the mausoleum in Bursa (1479) of Mehmet the Conqueror's son Mustafa, unusually well preserved.[8] Not only was the full range of cursive *thuluth* and square *kufic* scripts represented here, but there were also three colours in use: white, green and black. The scripts are sometimes mirror-imaged, sometimes superimposed, or sometimes lost among abstract decorative motifs that make them almost impossible to decipher. By the time of Sinan, clarity had come to the fore; the cursive *thuluth* script was preferred, and quotes from the Qur'an predominate.

Evliya Çelebi tells us that, in the quotes from the Qur'an that decorated the dome of the Süleymaniye Mosque, 'each *alif, lam* and *kaf* was made ten cubits tall in order to be easily read'.[9]

Inscriptions in earlier mosques had been a mix of Qur'anic passages together with quotations from the Hadith (sayings of the Prophet) and Persian poetry, an interesting glimpse into how differently the early Ottomans thought and the range of influences on them. By the time of Sinan, not only would a large percentage of the population of Istanbul have been literate, but the upper echelons of the elite would have been trilingual, reading Turkish, Arabic and Persian – all three of which are used in the foundation inscriptions of Sinan's mosques. Schools were abundant – there were 1,653 of them according to a 1577 census in Istanbul – and a Spanish slave observed that 'people who know how to read and write are by far more numerous' than in Spain.[10] The ninety-nine names of God were commonly used in Sinan's mosques at this time, along with the names of the four rightly guided caliphs, Abu Bakr, Umar, Uthman and Ali, all of which would have served as helpful reading aids for worshippers. Original wall painting from Sinan's time has been largely lost, overpainted by Baroque and Rococo designs, as have the original light fitments and decorative pendants including painted ostrich eggs. We do, however, have a visual description of the inside of the Selimiye Mosque in Edirne by a 16th-century German visitor, who saw 5,000 spherical mirrors and oil lamps, ranged as if to represent the strata of the heavens: 'Their dazzling reflection on those mirrors made the whole mosque appear as if it was on fire!'[11]

10
Architectural Identity

Origins and influences

Asked to visualize Ottoman architecture, most people will immediately think of the Istanbul skyline and the stereotype where slender mosque minarets spike the sky above vast, gently curving domes. Surrounded by water on three sides, it could hardly be further from the utter desolation of the Central Asian steppes, one of the bleakest and most waterless environments on the planet. The Oghuz tribesmen who formed the core of the early Ottomans knew the rigours of that life first hand. They would have longed for a homeland where water flowed in abundance and where their livestock could enjoy lush pastures: a paradise on earth.

When Mehmet the Conqueror took Constantinople, the city that the Turks had always referred to as 'the Red Apple', meaning the most coveted of all prizes, it was the realization of Osman's tree-based foundation dream. Small wonder, then, that the Ottomans chose the city, after brief periods in Bursa and Edirne, as their capital, which it remained for the next four and half centuries, and that they should have chosen the hilltop in Istanbul that commands views over all waterways as the location for the Topkapı Sarayı, their own discreet residence, surrounded by trees, gardens and water. Water was at the very core of the Ottoman architectural identity, just as it was also central to the many masterful works of the chief engineer Sinan, court architect to three sultans, whose work represents the Ottomans at their peak. It is no surprise either that the entrance to the inner courtyard of the Topkapı came to be known as the threshold to paradise – the *Bab al-Sa'ada*, literally the 'Gateway to Felicity', while the entrance to the outer courtyard was referred to as 'the Sublime Porte', the *Bab al-'Aali* (literally the 'High Gate'). Gateways have always held a special significance in Islamic architecture, with much decorative attention focused on them, often highlighted by contrasting bare walls. The phrase 'the Sublime Porte', or even just 'the Porte', came to refer in European diplomatic language to the Ottoman seat of government itself, as represented by the Topkapı Palace.

In Turkish mythology the relationship between heaven and earth is symbolized by means of a tree or mountain motif. Turks usually ascribed mystical or even divine values to large trees and forests, such as those in the Otuken forest. In Oghuz, Kipchak and Uygur legends, the birth of great men is always related to trees.[1] The tree of life represents the structure of the universe for peoples of Turkish origin, and an Altay folk song speaks of 'the iron mountain in the centre of the world and the white seven-branched tree on it'.[2]

Although Istanbul undoubtedly represents its architectural apogee, the origin of the Ottoman architectural identity goes much deeper. It has its roots in the structures designed for the Ottomans' very earliest communities in Bursa, the first capital, founded in 1326 (127 years before the conquest of Istanbul in 1453), and subsequently in Edirne, the second Ottoman capital from 1369 to 1453. It was in Bursa that the Ottomans developed an entirely new approach to urban design, from the bottom up, as it were, with the needs of the community placed firmly first, front and centre. Elaborate, expensive palaces constructed for the ruler could not have been further from the mind of the early Ottoman sultans, accustomed as they were to movable round tent homes.

When Mehmet the Conqueror captured Constantinople in 1453, he understood the importance of transforming Constantinople into an Ottoman city. He imported the best craftsmen, materials and builders from further east, and forced certain non-Turkic notables to come and settle there, knowing they would be vital to reviving the economy of the city and the empire. The conversion of Hagia Sophia into a mosque was easily accomplished, simply requiring the removal of the Christian decor and the adding of a *mihrab*, a *minbar* and rugs on the floor. Completed under the Emperor Justinian in 537, the structure was in poor condition at the time of the Muslim Conquest, but the Ottomans rebuilt and reinforced it with buttresses, adding its four minarets. It had been the religious centre of Orthodox Christianity and was the biggest church in the world. After 900 years as a church, and then 500 years as a mosque, it was turned into a museum in 1935 under Atatürk, until in 2020 it was converted back into a mosque by President Erdoğan. As a result the Hagia Sofia suffered from a significant loss of income from ticket sales, but the change was made for symbolic, not monetary, reasons.

Mehmet's own complex, known as the Fatih (meaning 'Conqueror'), was built from 1463 to 1470, and explicitly set out to rival the Hagia Sophia (see plate 20). The ambition to outdo the great church and its massive dome was foremost in the minds of many sultans and their architects. Mehmet's Fatih Mosque integrated elements from Romano-Byzantine and Italian Renaissance building traditions into an Ottoman framework to create a new style.[3] Contemporary written sources emphasized its heavenly symbolism: its eight *medreses*, for instance, were a reference to the eight gates of paradise. A further paradisiac feature, taken directly from Hagia Sophia, was the planting of four cypress trees, symbols of eternity, around the ablution fountain of the forecourt, a frequently repeated design in Istanbul's 16th-century mosques.

The Topkapı enigma

Visitors often ask why the Topkapı is so different from a grand European palace such as Versailles. Foreigners were consistently amazed at its horizontality, its relative modesty and its lack of monumentality and symmetry. At no point is it more than two stories tall. Mehmet the Conqueror ordered its construction in 1459, six years after his conquest of Constantinople. He took charge of the design himself, and one theory is that the layout, in which visitors pass through successive courtyards as they get closer and closer to the sultan, is a security measure aimed at providing him with maximum protection. At the same time it mirrored the arrangement of the early Ottoman tribal encampments, in which the *bey*'s tent is at the furthest point from the entrance and thus protected from sudden advances or enemy arrivals. Mehmet decided that his living quarters would be situated at the highest point of the promontory. The same spot had served as the acropolis of the Greek and Byzantine city of Byzantium, overlooking the Golden Horn where the Bosphorus Strait meets the Sea of Marmara, but the Great Palace of Constantinople was already largely in ruins when Mehmet took the city. A low-rise, sprawling complex, the First Court of the Topkapı is the largest and is also known as the 'Court of the Janissaries'. The Second Court would have been full of peacocks and gazelles, and was used as a gathering place for courtiers. The Gate of Felicity marks the entrance to the Third Court, or inner courtyard, which is where the private residential quarters were arranged and where no one was allowed to enter except with the express permission of the sultan. The Fourth Court is the innermost area, where the sultan could retreat with his family. Some walls of the palace are over 3 metres (10 feet) thick, which is why it was able to withstand the 1999 earthquake.

Opposite the kitchens, on the other side of the Second Court, is the Council Hall, which consists of three rooms roofed by three domes fronted by a portico. Difficult as it is to imagine, the entire empire was administered from these three very simple rooms. The first was the Grand Vizier Chamber, about 57 square metres (614 square feet) in size; the second, in the middle, was an inner treasury rather like a pantry under the responsibility of the treasurer, where money was stored in jars. The third was the imperial council chamber, known as the Kubbealtı. Adjoining these buildings is a door to the tower known as the Tower of Justice, and the door from the harem leading into the second courtyard. The sultans would enter the tower from the harem and listen in on discussions in the council chamber through a grille placed high in the wall.

The imperial stables underwent continual modifications over the years, so that in the 16th century some 300 servants were employed there, a number that had risen to 2,000 two centuries later. On top of the 300 stable servants, we are told there were 300 farriers, 300 saddlers, 2,000 muleteers, and enough camel drivers for 1,000 camels.[4]

The centrality of water in Ottoman architectural identity
Water of course has significance in all cultures – especially
Islamic cultures, in which ritual ablutions are performed five
times a day – but in Ottoman culture it assumed a special
importance, which in turn left its mark on Ottoman architecture. The Qur'an is full of numerous references to water, which
is seen both as life-giving and cleansing: 'We made every living
thing of water' (*Sura* 21, v. 30). The Ottomans adhered – like
the Moghuls of India – to the Hanafi school of Islamic law,
according to which ablutions had to be carried out not in a
communal basin of still, collected water, but under running
water (hence the word *hanafia*, which means 'tap' in Arabic).

In a cultural context where the life-giving and cleansing
properties of water were highly valued, running water was
the greatest thing a ruler or important individual could give
his subjects. In Islam, wealth is regarded as a possible danger
to the strict ideal of orthodox godliness – a spring of temp-
tation – which can be sanctioned only if the wealthy man
has identified his purpose as a donor and shared his wealth
with the poor. This was the reason for the ever-increasing
number of public buildings such as mosques, schools, caravanserais and baths, as well as beautifully designed fountains,
that began to grace Istanbul and many other Islamic cities.
Through giving, the rich man justified his wealth in the eyes
of God and his fellow beings. He created a monument but
was remembered as a benefactor. The *külliye* complex of the
Ottomans – a network of foundations that generated income
to maintain the mosque at its centre – was held to represent
the perfect balance between altruism and ambition. Istanbul
boasted dozens of *külliyes* at its height, and by the 18th century
these institutions were feeding some 30,000 people a day.[5]

Ottoman palaces had fountains from the beginning, and for the earliest, the Edirne Palace (*c.* 1425), very little of which survives today, we have a description by an early traveller of the unusual Cihannüma Kasrı ('Worldview' or 'Panorama' Pavilion) telling us that it was crowned with a strange octagonal observation tower. Testimony to the Ottoman love of heights, the building itself was seven stories high, rising some 70 feet (21 metres), and had 142 steps to the top. This may reflect the fact Edirne was low-lying, situated beside a river and lacked the naturally hilly terrain of Istanbul. Inside, the observation room, known as the 'Imperial Sultan's Throne Room', was tiled with marble and, despite the presumably difficult installation, had an internal fountain.[6] The rest of the building housed a library, a reception room and a mosque. Other structures within the palace grounds included a bathhouse, the imperial kitchens, a hunting lodge, and a tower of justice, all of which mirror later structures within the Topkapı Palace. Like the Topkapı, it even had its own 'Gate of Felicity', still partially standing. Work is ongoing to restore the palace and the unique observation tower after it was destroyed in the 1877–78 Russo-Turkish war. A photo of it still exists, taken by a Russian army intelligence officer.

One of Mehmet the Conqueror's first acts after the conquest of Constantinople in 1453 was to restore its neglected Byzantine pipework and to renovate the failing Roman Aqueduct of Valens; his aim was to bring in water from the Belgrade Forest to the north-west so that he could create a large new public cistern.

At the start of Süleyman the Magnificent's reign in 1520, the capital had a population of 100,000, and it was growing. As a result, there was an urgent need to improve and extend the city's water supply, in order to keep the residents happy, to avoid rebellions and to enable the city to continue its growth.

Süleyman and his architect, Sinan

It was fortunate for both the city and the sultan that Sinan appeared on the scene at this precise point, having worked his way up through the *devşirme* system and having gained much experience of building bridges as well as a deep understanding of the complexities of designing water systems. Becoming court architect in 1538, he was responsible for repairs to and the maintenance of the existing dams, cisterns and aqueducts and for the water supply systems that fed all the capital's imperial buildings, from mosques and *medreses* to hammams and palaces. So vital was this work that the post of Inspector of Waterworks (*Suyolu Nazırı*) was created in 1566; the incumbent was charged with the construction and maintenance of urban water supplies across the empire. This crucial position came to be seen as the stepping stone to higher posts, and all three of Sinan's successors in the role went to become court architects themselves. The two officials generally worked alongside each other, as at the 18th-century Baroque-style Nurosmaniye Mosque, for example, where the floor of the mosque was raised on a basement of great piers, since the digging of the foundations had taken them below the water table.

Under Süleyman, Sinan began the construction of a new and much-extended water supply system for Istanbul in 1554 that was to take ten years to complete. Before beginning the actual construction, Sinan conducted a great deal of fieldwork, personally exploring the areas above the two major rivers that flow into the Golden Horn in search of remnants of the ancient Roman water system. Wherever possible he reused the old system, diverting rivers into aqueducts and studying the topography, to conduct the water into the capital in the most efficient way. Before its completion, water could be drawn from over 300 wells in the capital. By the time he finished working on the new system, it could be drawn from 5,901, a fact that would have greatly enhanced the city's reputation, as a city's wealth was generally measured according to the number of wells or hammams that a city could afford to maintain. The sultan also enhanced his own reputation by endowing public fountains that distributed free drinking water, thus providing both a blessing and focal point for the neighbourhood.

Over his lifetime Sinan built three major water systems, each totalling about 50 kilometres (30 miles) in length. The first was built in Edirne around 1530, when Sinan was 40, before he was court architect, then extended in 1554 and 1574. Called the Taşlımüsellim, it is still in partial operation. Its capacity of about 3,000 cubic metres (660,000 gallons) a day was collected from two springs and then fed into one channel over 20 kilometres (12½ miles) long, which incorporated five tunnels and twelve aqueducts. His second water system was built between 1550 and 1557 (when Sinan was in his sixties) specifically for the Süleymaniye and was the largest of fifteen separate water systems arriving from the north-west of Istanbul. The channel travelled through tunnels and over aqueducts, enabling the water to cross hilly topography along ancient Roman systems before terminating in the courtyard of the Süleymaniye, where it cascaded from the roof of the elegantly carved marble central fountain, before being channelled off towards the separate ablution area along the outer wall.

Sinan's third and greatest water system was the Kırkçeşme (Forty Springs), fed by springs in the Belgrade Forest. Originally the hunting ground of the Ottomans, the Belgrade Forest is the largest wooded area in the vicinity of Istanbul and still a popular escape from the city for today's residents. Its name comes from the people of Belgrade who were settled here after the Ottoman conquest and whose job it was to look after the reservoirs supplying the city, along with the dams, water towers and aqueducts. Today it still supplies a capacity of 10,000 cubic metres (2.2 million gallons) of water a day, which is carried across several extremely fine aqueducts, notably the Uzun and the Mağlova. The latter is generally rated as Sinan's most beautiful, described by European travellers in 19th century as 'Justinian's Aqueduct', even though it is not Roman.[7] The same occurred with the Ottoman bridge at Mostar in the Balkans, which was persistently labelled 'Roman' by European historians because only the Romans, and certainly not the Turks, were deemed capable of building such splendid bridges.

After his death in 1588, Sinan's own mausoleum was built in a beautiful enclosure of latticed stone beside his residence, in a lower corner of the gigantic Süleymaniye complex. This was a unique privilege and an acknowledgment of Sinan's status, as was the original grant of land in such a significant location for his two-storey, three-courtyard residence, with its two bathhouses and five toilets.[8] Carved into the stone above the tomb's iron-grilled prayer window – alongside a public fountain, facing out to the street and designed to be read by all passers-by – is the following inscription in Ottoman Turkish:

O you, who settle for a day or two in life's palace,
The world is not a place of repose for man.
Becoming the architect of Süleyman Khan,
   this distinguished man
Built him a Friday mosque that is a sign of the
   highest paradise.
With the sultan's orders he exerted great effort on
   water channels,

Like Hızır,[9] *he made the water of life flow to the people.*
At the [Büyük] Çekmece bridge such a lofty arch did he
    raise that
Identical it is to the form of the Milky Way in the mirror
    of Time.
He built more than four hundred lofty masjids,
Creating Friday mosques in eighty places, this divine maestro.
He lived more than a hundred years and finally passed away;
May God make his resting place the garden of paradise.[10]

The words are written by Mustafa Sai, the poet and painter of the day, to whom Sinan dictated his autobiography. Given the extent to which Sinan wished to be remembered by posterity and the care he took over his autobiography, it would be only natural to assume that the emphasis these verses give to Sinan's achievements in the realm of water systems is a fair reflection of his own assessment of their importance. Water infuses the conscious symbolism of his architecture. Sinan's biographer, Sai, compares the multiple domes of the Şehzade and Süleymaniye complexes to 'bubbles on the surface of the sea',[11] and the Sokullu Mehmet Mosque's *waqf* document describes the appearance of the mosque's 'sumptuous and soaring dome' as 'a pleasant bubble on the lip of the sea'.

Types of fountain

The Ottomans endowed different kinds of fountain, examples of which can be found in towns and villages throughout the empire, though of course they are at their most numerous in Istanbul. The first-ever Ottoman fountain was thought to be at the Murad I Mosque in Bursa, a simple hexagonal ablution fountain in the centre of the courtyard. The most basic type was the *çeşme*, Turkish for spring or well, which was installed in residential districts for people to come and collect water for use in their homes. These were provided by the city waterworks administration. The second type was the *sebil* or *sebilhane*, a water dispenser that generally stood in more prestigious parts of town and was endowed as an act of piety by a local benefactor (perhaps an official, a vizier or even the sultan himself). The third type was the *şadırvan*, an ornamental fountain or tank decorating the courtyard of a mosque, or, as in the case of the Süleymaniye, doubling as the central reservoir for the internal water supply. The height of the platform Sinan built for the Süleymaniye and the exact siting of the fountains would have had to be among the first decisions he took in its planning. Unique in Ottoman architecture, the mosque's elegant rectangular *şadırvan* was carved from beautiful white marble, and the water was fed onto its roof, from which it plunged constantly in ever cascading streams. Writing in 1573, the French diplomat Philippe de La Canaye described it as 'dignified enough to be compared with the most famous grottoes of Naples'. Admiring its design, he noted that 'thanks to a cunning artifice water falls like rain into a square basin of marble'.[12] In Sinan's autobiography it is compared to the pool of paradise, and Sinan himself singles it out as one of his best artistic inventions.[13]

Sinan's own love of water and fountains is clear from his well-watered residence and the drinking fountain beside his tomb. During his lifetime he received complaints in the form of anonymous petitions sent to Murad III in 1577 accusing him of illegally diverting water from the Süleymaniye complex for his own use.[14] He also personally endowed three fountains near his birthplace at Kayseri, in modern Cappadocia.

Süleyman became renowned for sponsoring a series of monumental architectural developments within his empire. He sought to turn Constantinople into the centre of Islamic civilization through a succession of projects, including bridges, mosques, palaces and various charitable and social establishments. Sinan in turn was responsible for over 300 monuments throughout the Ottoman territories. Süleyman also restored the Dome of the Rock in Jerusalem and the city walls (which are the current walls of the old city), renovated the Kaaba in Mecca, and constructed a *külliye* complex in Damascus.

In Edirne, Sinan built what he considered his masterpiece, the Selimiye Mosque complex (1568–75). On its completion, he is said to have exclaimed: 'Justinian, I have outdone you!' – a reference to the Byzantine emperor's triumph with the Hagia Sophia. The Selimiye was managed as a single institution and included *medreses*, a covered market, a clock house, an outer courtyard and a library. Registered as a UNESCO World Heritage site in 2011, it dominates the skyline of Edirne with its four soaring, slender minarets, single great dome, meticulous craftsmanship and superb Iznik tiles. Its innovative structural design allows for numerous windows, which create an extraordinary illuminated interior. The UNESCO entry cites it as 'the apogee of an art form and the pious benefaction of 16th century imperial Islam ... the most harmonious expression ever achieved of the *külliye*, this most peculiarly Ottoman type of complex'.[15]

Ottoman Baroque fountains

Like an orchestra playing on a sinking ship, the brief so-called 'Tulip Period' (1718–30) gave rise to a flurry of extravagant buildings in Istanbul almost in defiance of the reality of the empire's decline and its political struggles following defeats by the Habsburg Austrians. These structures represented an inverse barometer of the times, in that they became ever more elaborate as the empire's power dwindled. The expensive cultivation of the tulip appeared to provide a welcome distraction from the losses the empire suffered. A major reorientation towards the West was beginning; and, when the army was also heavily defeated in Persia, Ahmet III was forced to abdicate in 1730 and the Tulip Period came to an abrupt end. No large mosque complexes were built during this period (just one small *medrese* complex, built by Ahmet III's vizier in 1719–20), since raw materials and financial means were scarce. Fountains began to increase in importance and visibility, becoming free-standing structures of great elegance and complexity in their own right rather than simply part of other complexes. They stood in prominent places in the city, often in the vicinity of tombs, delivering water from the reservoir; the water was dispensed either by a ladling man from the inside room or directly from drinking fountains set into the outer walls. They also became places where the pious might offer prayers in remembrance of the fountain's benefactor and were often covered in inscriptions in his praise or quotes from poetic verse.

Ottoman dams and bridges

The constantly expanding population meant that the Istanbul's water supply had to be increased, something that was achieved through the construction of a series of very fine dams that, by the 19th century, had evolved into constructions reinforced with piers that were ahead of anything else in Europe. They were also designed to be recreational areas where residents of the city could come out to stroll: they were designed like promenades, with marble banisters, and some even had little balconies where shades could be erected against the sun. That of Mahmud II, inaugurated in 1839, represents the peak of Ottoman dam construction.

Tiles in Ottoman architecture

The use of stunningly colourful Iznik tiles as wall coverings is a distinctive Ottoman feature but did not begin in earnest until after the 1453 conquest of Constantinople. It developed at speed in response to an imperial decree requisitioning vast quantities of tiles to decorate the interiors of the new Ottoman buildings, especially those commissioned by Süleyman and designed by Sinan. The Ottoman traveller Evliya Çelebi recorded seeing over 300 tile workshops in the city of Iznik, where the availability of the right kind of clay, water from the lake and wood for the furnaces made it a perfect location.[16] The most beautiful examples of Iznik tiles are all to be found in Istanbul: at the Topkapı Palace, especially in the harem; at Süleyman and Roxelana's tombs within the Süleymaniye Mosque complex; at the Rüstem Pasha Mosque within the Egyptian Spice Bazaar; at the Sokullu Mehmet Mosque, near the Blue Mosque; and at Sultan Ahmet's Blue Mosque, where the tiles feature over fifty different tulip designs.

The Balkans

Although the Ottoman architectural legacy can be seen all over the Balkans, attitudes towards it differ from country to country. As might be expected, the countries that today have large majority Muslim populations, such as Albania, Kosovo, Bosnia and Herzegovina, and North Macedonia, view the Ottoman heritage most favourably and still have many mosques in use. In majority Christian countries, like Serbia and Bulgaria, attitudes are much more hostile: far more mosques are abandoned or in a state of disrepair. In Albania, where the Muslim population today is estimated at roughly 60 per cent, the Ottomans were first invited in by an Albanian noble in 1385. The country played a prestigious role in Ottoman history throughout the 17th, 18th and 19th centuries, remaining part of the empire until 1912, yet the dearth of mosques is striking. Some 2,000 of them were destroyed under the former Communist regime, and interest in the country's Ottoman heritage among Albania's population today is minimal.

Greece

In Greece, cities such as Thessalonica, Kavala, Giannitsa, Serres and Trikola are interesting because they had such diverse populations in Ottoman times. Thessalonica boasted the world's largest and only Jewish-majority city in the 16th century, while the others were roughly half Christian, half Muslim. Mosques and hammams were built, and the Ottomans constructed the same water systems as in Istanbul to bring in water, together with public fountains to provide drinking water.

Kavala was the birthplace of Muhammad Ali, an Albanian Ottoman military commander who went on to found his own breakaway dynasty in Egypt in 1805, ruling it until his death in 1848. He is widely seen as the founder of modern Egypt, and his house in Kavala has been preserved as a museum. He endowed his native town with an astonishing *külliye* complex built over a thirteen-year period, from 1808 to 1821. As well as a mosque that doubled as a lecture hall, a *medrese*, a primary school, a library and a soup kitchen to feed the students and teachers, it included a 'Charitable College of Engineering'

(Mühandeshane-i Hayriyye) and had sixty rooms to accommodate its students. Documents that shed light on the political, economic and religious background to this huge complex have recently emerged from the Egyptian National Archives in another example of how Ottoman-era material is increasingly being uncovered by a new generation of scholars. The complex was restored in 2001–4.

A scholar working on a PhD thesis that looks at Ottoman heritage in Greece and Byzantine heritage in Turkey recently sent questionnaires to the inhabitants of Serres and Trikola in Greece. He found that most educated people felt that it was the duty of everyone to look after cultural heritage, except in the case of Ottoman cultural heritage, which they did not feel was their responsibility: they did not consider Ottoman monuments to be part of their national identity.[17] Former mosques in Greece have tended to be abandoned, but some hammams have been converted into exhibition spaces.

Bosnia

In Bosnia, where the population is over 50 per cent Muslim, most of the country's Ottoman architecture is concentrated in Sarajevo, the capital. Built by the Ottomans, it is sometimes called 'the Jerusalem of Europe' and is one of the very few cities to boast a mosque, a Catholic church, an Orthodox church and a synagogue all within the same neighbourhood. The city's oldest synagogue, built in 1581, today serves as the Jewish Museum of Bosnia and Herzegovina. Sarajevo's multicultural identity has earned it a place on UNESCO's Tentative List, along with the stunning nearby Sufi lodge at Blagaj.

It was the Ottomans who built the main mosque in Sarajevo, and also the Orthodox church beside it, which is smaller and more discreet, but still very close, so that congregations could mingle, even though the dominance of the mosque is clear.

Sinan's bridge across the Drina River at Višegrad, with its eleven masonry arches and elegant proportions, represents the apogee of Ottoman monumental architecture and civil engineering. It was designated a UNESCO World Heritage site in 2007.

Bosnia's other famous bridge, inscribed on the UNESCO list in 2005, stands in the historic town of Mostar, spanning a deep valley of the Neretva River. Mostar developed in the 15th and 16th centuries as an Ottoman frontier town and has long been known for its old Turkish houses and the Old Bridge (Stari Most), after which the town is named. Blown up in the 1990s Balkan conflict, the Old Bridge was rebuilt in 2004, along with many of the historic buildings. Today the old town's narrow, cobbled streets are lined with bazaars bursting with Turkish tourist souvenirs, while restaurants overlooking the gorge offer Turkish delicacies and 'Bosnian' coffee.

North Macedonia

North Macedonia is one-third Muslim, two-thirds Orthodox Christian – a proportion reflected in the 580 mosques and 1,842 churches recorded in the country in 2011. Skopje, the capital, boasts a fine Ottoman stone bridge, together with a fully functioning bazaar, mosques and hammams.

Bulgaria

The case of Bulgaria is an interesting one. The country is overwhelmingly Christian (around 70 per cent) and determined to wipe out any traces of Ottoman influence. Yet ironically, what is termed 'Bulgarian national revival architecture' is very obviously derived from its centuries of exposure to Ottoman culture. The Bulgarian Orthodox Church has suffered a serious decline since 2001, its credibility much undermined by its collaboration with the erstwhile Communist regime.

Rila Monastery, the largest and most famous Orthodox monastery in Bulgaria, still houses about sixty monks, yet the country's many centuries of Ottoman rule (1400–1878) again show themselves in the porticos of the courtyard, with their striped arches, and the domes of the church, which became more popular in the Ottoman Empire after the conquest of Egypt.

Serbia

Serbia is majority Orthodox Christian, at 86 percent; just 3 per cent of the population is Muslim, most of whom are concentrated in Novi Pazar in the extreme south-west, a town that still feels entirely Muslim. Turkey is said to be funding the restoration of some its mosques.

Arab provinces

Syria

The story of the Ottomans' architectural legacy is very different in the former Arab provinces, where the population remains overwhelmingly Muslim, with Christian minorities of around 10 per cent in both Syria and Egypt. The Ottoman province of Syria was much bigger than today's amputated state and included present-day Lebanon, Jordan, Israel, and Palestine and the Holy Land, right down to Sinai. Damascus surrendered to the Ottomans on 3 October 1516 with no resistance – except, initially, from the Mamluk governor of the citadel. The sultan himself, Selim the Resolute, was so relaxed about the takeover of the city that he stopped for a bath and a shave at a hammam just north of the walls.

Over the course of the four centuries of Ottoman rule, Damascus finally outgrew the walled space of the Old City that had served it for two to three thousand years. The gradual modernizing process that took place drew the centre inexorably westwards, with the later law courts, banks, bus and rail stations, education and publishing houses all based to that side. Most of the commercial activities, however, remained concentrated inside the walls, with the 18th century in particular seeing a massive burgeoning of khans, as the city's trade beyond its borders entered a period of great prosperity and growth. Allied to that prosperity, was a parallel burgeoning of residential architecture, with very grand private courtyard houses like Bait al-'Azem, Bait Nizam and Bait al-Siba'i.

THE IBN 'ARABI MOSQUE

The first building that Selim ordered to be constructed after the surrender of Damascus was a new mosque over the existing tomb of Sheikh Muhyi Al-Din, a much-revered Sufi of Andalusian origin, popularly known as Ibn 'Arabi, who died in Damascus in 1240. The Ottomans were keen to associate themselves with such a popular shrine, knowing it would facilitate their acceptance by the local population. This, the first Ottoman complex to be built in Damascus – on the slopes of Mount Qassioun, in the northern district of Salihiyya overlooking the city – comprised a mosque, a mausoleum (*türbe*) and a *tekkiye*, or Sufi monastery. It was constructed in the remarkably short timeframe of five months, so that the sultan could be present at the opening, and became the most important religious complex in the city after the Great Umayyad Mosque, eclipsing all earlier pious foundations. The sum of 10,000 dinars was paid to an Ottoman administrator to manage the construction, and the income from seven villages was earmarked as a *waqf* to cover the expenses incurred in operating and maintaining the buildings. On 5 February 1518 Selim I celebrated the first Friday prayers in the new mosque – the first Friday of Ramadan. Today the mosque still stands beside a bustling market, Souq Al-Jum'a, so-called because it is the only one in the city open on Fridays.

Lining the walls of the *türbe* to a height of over 5 metres (16 feet) and especially impressive on the eastern party wall with the mosque are beautiful ceramic tiles that represent a wonderful blending of the Damascus and Ottoman styles. The boldly drawn flowers appear in perpetual bloom, evoking the gardens of paradise, while cypress trees, highly prized as motifs, emphasize the architectural verticality of the building.

THE TEKKIYE SÜLEYMANIYE

This later landmark building, built under the reign of Süleyman the Magnificent, was an imperial project intended to establish the religious credentials of the Ottomans as guardians of pilgrims preparing for their journey to Mecca. Possession of and responsibility for the sacred sites of Islamic orthodoxy imbued the Ottomans with greater legitimacy. The location of the monastery, on the banks of the Barada, was where pilgrims traditionally gathered, resting and stocking up with provisions to take with them on the 35-day journey across the desert. According to Jacques de Villamont, a French traveller who visited in 1590, it was remarkable place:

> A quarter of a mile from Damascus lies a very beautiful khan named Tacheye [*takiyya*], built by Sulayman Sultan, father of the great Turk who now reigns, to lodge all the Muslim pilgrims who travel to Mecca to visit the sepulchre of Mahomet and to feed them, and likewise their horses and camels for a space of

three days without them paying a penny, though if one stays longer, one has to pay one's own board. These lodgings are well built and very pleasant owing to their beautiful garden and the fine arched galleries surrounding it ... In the middle of the yard, there is a fountain with excellent water, of which each drinks as he will, and all these buildings are made in a square shape and are all roofed in lead, as too is the adjoining mosque ... In this khan, Christians are as well received and nourished for three days like Turks, since Turkish charity extends to all, irrespective of religion.[18]

In later centuries Istanbul found itself distracted by problems including tribal uprisings and political challenges in Europe, so Syria fell down the scale of priorities once the pilgrimage had been tended to each year. Most of Damascus's subsequent Ottoman mosques were therefore the work of local governors. Mindful of the dangers these individuals might pose if they were left in power for too long, the authorities in Istanbul adopted a policy of changing governors regularly, so that in practice they often governed for no more than a year or two.

Lebanon

The Grand Serail in Beirut, built in the 19th century, still serves today as the headquarters of the Lebanese prime minister, and various other Ottoman-era buildings have miraculously survived the city's devastating civil war, including the distinctive Moorish-revival Hamadiyyah Clock Tower (1897).

The country's most beautiful Ottoman-era relic, however, is the stunning Beiteddine Palace, built in the 18th and 19th centuries high in the Chouf mountains south of Beirut. Since 1943 it has served as the president's official summer residence. Badly damaged during the 1975–1990 civil war, it has been well restored and is open to the public, as well as providing an unforgettable venue for the annual Beiteddine Festival.[19]

Lebanon's Mediterranean ports of Tripoli, Sidon and Tyre were all vital Ottoman trading centres and retain their Ottoman-era khans and souks in the heart of the old cities. Süleyman the Magnificent restored Tripoli's citadel, a former 12th-century Crusader castle, after his father, Selim the Resolute, captured the province of Syria, out of which Lebanon was carved by the French in 1920 after the Ottoman demise. Inscribed above the gateway is Süleyman's inscription:

> In the name of Allah, it has been decreed by the royal sultan's order, al Malik al-Muzuffar Sultan Suleiman Shah, son of Sultan Selim Shah, may his orders never cease to be obeyed by the emirs, that this blessed citadel be restored so as to be a fortified stronghold for all time. Its construction was completed in the blessed month of Sha'bân of the year 927 [July 1521].

Egypt

In Cairo, the first example of Ottoman architecture was the mosque of Süleyman Pasha al-Khadim, built at the citadel in 1528 to serve the janissaries. It has a classic central-domed plan with pencil minaret but was quite unlike anything seen in Cairo before. The janissaries were stationed at the citadel, the base from which they were in charge of the whole of the province of Egypt. Dominating the city skyline from the citadel's highest point is the instantly recognizable Ottoman profile of the huge Muhammad Ali Mosque, with its twin minarets (1848) – a landmark attraction for today's visitors. Built in the style of his former overlords and modelled on Istanbul's 1616 Sultan Ahmet Mosque (the Blue Mosque), it shows that Muhammad Ali, who chose to be buried there, remained an Ottoman at heart. Otherwise the main Ottoman buildings in Cairo were fountains, including a fine example in the heart of the old city, completed in 1744 and quite new in style.

Ottoman tiles were not restricted to Muslim buildings but reached even as far as St Catherine's Monastery in Sinai.

Iraq

Baghdad still has the al-Wazir Mosque, built in 1660 on the banks of the Tigris, and the al-Maqam Mosque in Basra, dating back to 1754, both of which have been restored over the years and are still in use.

Algeria

There are still visible remnants of the Ottoman legacy in Algeria, particularly in Algiers and above all in the Kasbah in the heart of the city. Under French rule, the Algerians expressed their distinct national identity by putting Islamic patterns on buildings such as the Post Office. The medina boasted 50 hammams and 150 fountains. Today shops in the Kasbah still sell beautiful colourful lamps of the type popularized under Ottoman rule.

Contemporary interpretations

The principles of Ottoman architecture live on in Turkey today thanks to modern architects such as Alpaslan Ataman, who died in 2020. He pioneered a system that analysed the planning and organization of Ottoman architecture based on its unique spatial typologies and geometrics. He then applied the lessons of Ottoman urbanism to our modern world, and believed that key buildings such as mosques and churches should be incorporated into the fabric of a city, so that they reveal themselves step by step, rather than appear all of a sudden in a cleared space.[20]

11
Culinary Delights

HOW PROSAIC WESTERN food seems when compared to the exoticism of Ottoman cuisine. The original Western fast food, the sandwich, was named after the 18th-century Earl of Sandwich who liked to eat meat between two slices of bread when playing lengthy games of cards. Ottoman chefs, on the other hand, who were always male, let their fantasies run wild with creations including 'women's thighs' (minced spiced lamb rolled into long round shapes), 'lady's navel' and 'beauty's lip' (both rich sweets).

Recognized as one of the world's great cuisines, alongside French and Chinese, the culinary legacy of the Ottomans is enormous, extending to places as far apart as Pakistan and North America. Some names we use every day for certain foods, such as yogurt, baklava and kebab, bear witness to their Turkish origins, though many are misappropriated by other nations. Turkish coffee, for instance, is claimed by virtually every Balkan country as well as the Arab provinces: reincarnated as 'Greek coffee', 'Albanian coffee', 'Arab coffee', 'Bulgarian coffee' and so on, both in speech and on menus, it is unmistakably based on the same drink and accompanies the same rituals of friendship and hospitality.

On his travels through the Habsburg borderlands in the mid-17th century, Evliya Çelebi was not impressed with Western dining: 'Actually, none of the food throughout Christendom is worthy of note. The infidels are abstemious at mealtimes, eating fifty drams of food from the tip of an iron fork, and sipping fifty drams of wine. Dining is only found in the Ottoman Empire. Nor is there any cuisine to speak of in India and Persia – only their pilavs are worth mentioning.'[1]

In the enormous kitchens of the Topkapı Palace, some 20,000 sheep and poultry were slaughtered every year. Sixty cooks were employed, including twelve cooks for the sultan's private kitchen. Fifty sheep and four or five cattle were slaughtered every day.[2] Süleyman the Magnificent ate his meals off exquisite Chinese plates, and by the 18th century the palace inventories registered more than 8,000 items of oriental ceramics. It is testimony to the strength of this tradition that Istanbul boasts the most important collections of Chinese porcelain outside of China.

As with so much in Ottoman culture, it was the Seljuks, the Ottomans' Turkic predecessors, who provided the foundation of many elements that would come to define their cuisine. A nomadic people, the Seljuks had lived mainly on meat and dairy produce from their livestock, but they left their nomadic lifestyle behind and began to grow many what would become staple crops for the Ottomans, such as rice, wheat, barley and millet. Apples, grapes, watermelons and berries became their favourite fruits. The Seljuks' conversion to Islam brought with it strict guidelines on what could not be consumed – pork, alcohol and certain types of seafood were forbidden – another factor that influenced the development of dishes.

Bread was a mainstay of the Ottoman diet, and Evliya Çelebi records that there were forty-six varieties of bread within the empire (see plate 21). It was eaten at both main meals of the day, especially alongside stews and broths, and was accompanied by numerous spreads. One such, made from chickpeas, cinnamon and pine nuts, is thought to be the ancestor of the ubiquitous modern-day hummus. When it came to pastries, the Ottoman favourite was *börek*, small, flaky, savoury parcels shaped like triangles or cigars and filled with meat, cheese and vegetables, often mixed with dried fruits.

Lamb and chicken were the favourite meats, roasted whole or chopped and made into the kebabs for which the region is still famous today. Wrapped meat and stuffing are another staple, with the commonest form of *dolma* (Turkish for 'stuffed') being the stuffed vine leaves usually claimed by Greek cuisine, though cabbage leaves, green peppers, aubergines and cour-gettes were also stuffed with meat-based fillings. *Ayva dolma*, or stuffed quinces, appear in a dish believed to have originated in the palace kitchen, now a rare but succulent speciality in some parts of the former Ottoman Empire.

Rich desserts included multi-layered pastry interlaced with layers of honey, known as baklava: it is eaten throughout the world today and is thought to be the origin of the German strudel. In the 15th and 16th centuries baklava was eaten only by the elite of Ottoman society, its recipe closely guarded within the walls of the palace. Sherbet was another Ottoman favourite, in which a rich syrup (from which the name comes) made from boiled fruit was drunk on special occasions or to revive weary travellers. The French in the 1800s developed it into sorbet, the frozen water ice still used as a palate cleanser between courses, while the Germans and especially the English went further: chemists discovered an exotic fizzy powder version immortalized forever in children's sweets.[3] Nuts are an essen-tial ingredient in Turkish desserts, and to this day Turkey is the world's biggest producer of hazelnuts, making up 75 per cent of the market share, and one of the biggest producers of pistachios, walnuts and almonds.

Ottoman palace cuisine under Süleyman and his successors was highly refined but largely secret. No recipes were ever written down. The diverse cuisine was perfected in the imperial palace kitchens by chefs brought from various parts of the empire for the express purpose of inventing new dishes and experimenting with exotic textures and ingredients. All dishes intended for the sultan were first checked by the palate of the Chesnidjibashi, or imperial food taster, who tested the food for both poison and flavour. A few creations from the palace kitchens filtered down to the common population, but the vast bulk are lost to posterity. We know, however, that each cook had his own speciality in the preparation of the complex recipes. At the dissolution of the empire the cooks dispersed, taking their knowledge with them.

Food for the army

The phenomenal success of the Ottomans in war and conquest up till the late 17th century must in part be linked to their exceptional command of logistics and their ability to provide a sophisticated food supply chain for their armies, making sure nutritious, morale-boosting food was always available. Grain stores were kept constantly filled in peacetime, and during the campaign season, from early spring to late autumn, bread was baked en masse in advance of the army. Special divisions were responsible for fresh water supplies for both men and pack animals, while others took care of perishable foods. Two meals a day was the norm, with generous rations of bread, meat and rice often made into nutritious broths, only slightly simplified compared with what the troops would have eaten at home.

Well-fed soldiers were less likely to pillage food from the local populations, which risked starting a revolt and stirring up antagonism.

Ottoman drinks

Coffee

The popularity of coffee across the Ottoman Empire goes back to the 1550s, when the first coffee shop was opened in Istanbul by two Yemenis during the reign of Süleyman the Magnificent, himself a great lover of the drink. He instituted the position of 'Chief Coffee Maker', who was responsible for preparing the sultan's coffee and the utensils needed to make the perfect product. The furniture of Ottoman palaces evolved to enable guests to enjoy the coffee ritual. Guests sat on a low bench or divan built against the wall while trays of food and drink were set before them on beautifully decorated tables. Once such table, dating from 1560, is on display in London's Victoria and Albert Museum: made of ebony and faced with mother of pearl and ivory inlay, it is topped with exquisite Iznik tiles. The kilns of Kütahya, south of Iznik, were also kept busy producing beautifully decorated coffee cups, some of which can also be seen in the same collection.

Before reaching the Ottoman capital, coffee had arrived in Syria in 1534 from Moccha in Yemen, but in 1546 it was banned at the behest of the Ottoman authorities and certain pious muftis who considered its influence to be suspect, fearing that coffee-houses would become places for disreputable practices. Previous attempts had also been made to ban it in Mecca and Cairo. The first recorded coffee-houses in Damascus were located on the banks of the Barada near the Tekkiye Süleymaniye (Süleyman's dervish lodge) and could house hundreds of customers at a time, often pilgrims gathering for the Hajj. Only one survives from that early phase: the Café Nawfara at the eastern gateway to the Temple of Jupiter, today the Great Umayyad Mosque. By the end of the 16th century there were some 600 coffee-houses in Istanbul, a number that rose to 2,500 by the end of the 19th century, when the introduction of tea demoted it to second place as the favourite drink across the empire.

Coffee was introduced to France with the 1669 visit of the Turkish ambassador Süleyman Aga to the court of Louis XIV.[4] Consumed in Europe in the traditional Muslim way, it was made by boiling a mixture of coffee powder, sugar and water, which left a residue in the bottom of the cup because it was not filtered (what we today still call 'Turkish coffee'). Coffee reached the Austro-Hungarian Empire in 1683 following the siege of Vienna by a huge and well-equipped Ottoman army under the command of the grand vizier Kara Mustafa. After months of bombardment, and just as the fortifications of the city seemed to be giving way, the siege was lifted owing to the arrival of forces under Prince Sobieski of Poland and Charles, Duke of Lorraine. In a remarkable reversal, the besieging Ottoman army was routed and its entire camp captured, including almost all its armaments and provisions. Viennese officials were amazed at the copious amounts of material and foodstuffs the camp contained, especially the 'prodigious stores of victuals'. In their inventory of the spoils, the Viennese chroniclers listed coffee beans among the grain, flour, butter, bread, lard, rice, sugar, honey, cooking oil and kitchenware, as well as live camels, buffaloes, mules, oxen and sheep. The starving Viennese must have feasted for days. One Polish officer was rewarded for his bravery in undertaking dangerous espionage during the battle with bags of coffee beans, which no one had any idea how to use.

The officer was said to have been an Ottoman prisoner for two years and therefore knew what to do with them; he was able to sell coffee to the Viennese citizenry, giving them a taste for the distinctive drink. The first actual Viennese coffee-house was not opened until 1685, by a canny Armenian merchant who had applied for and been granted the sole privilege of preparing and offering for sale 'the Oriental drink' for a period of twenty years. Thereafter the sale of coffee remained carefully controlled in the city, so that by 1729 there were still only eleven licensed concessionaires.[5]

A Turkish merchant in 1650 was the first to bring coffee commercially into the United Kingdom, selling it in a coffee-house in George Yard, Lombard Street, London. Another café called the 'Sultaness Head' opened eight years later in Cornhill. The insurance company Lloyd's of London was originally a coffee shop called 'Edward Lloyd's Coffee House'. By 1700 there were around 500 coffee-houses in London and nearly 3,000 in the whole of England. They were known as 'penny universities' because you could listen and talk to the great minds of the day for the price of a coffee, which cost one penny.

In the Ottoman Empire the drinking of coffee was a controversial issue: aside from the stimulating properties of the drink itself, coffee-houses were seen as meeting places that challenged the traditional role of mosques. In the mid-1500s, many ships' cargoes of coffee beans were tipped into the sea. The drink was the subject of an Ottoman treatise by Sarı Mehmet Pasha, treasurer to Ahmet III (r. 1703–30), in which he explained how coffee first came to Anatolia by sea and met with a hostile reception:

> But these strictures and prohibitions availed nothing.
> The fatwas, the talk, made no impression on the people.
> One coffee-house was opened after another, and men would
> gather together, with great eagerness and enthusiasm, to

drink ... To those of dry temperament, especially to the
man of melancholic temperament, large quantities are
unsuitable, and may be repugnant. Taken in excess, it
causes insomnia and melancholic anxiety. If drunk at all,
it should be drunk with sugar. To those of moist temperament,
and especially of women, it is highly suited. They should drink
a great deal of strong coffee. Excess of it will do them no harm,
so long as they are not melancholic.[6]

Public coffee-houses did indeed play a role as meeting places for different groups of people depending on their locations. Those frequented by craftsmen tended to be located in Fatih, Beyazıt and Sirkeçi, for instance, while many janissaries opened their own establishments to supplement their salaries. Some had live singers, some had storytellers, and others became known as venues where intellectuals discussed politics. At times of unrest, Ottoman rulers would close such places down to stop people plotting subterfuge. One 17th-century Ottoman chronicler wrote:

These shops became meeting-places of a circle of pleasure-
seekers and idlers, and also of some wits from among the men
of letters and literati, and they used to meet in groups of about
twenty or thirty. Some read books and fine writings, some
were busy with backgammon and chess, some brought new
poems and talked of literature.[7]

Attempts to shut the coffee-houses simply meant that they moved to backstreets and alleys, but the authorities finally accepted them, not least since they were important sources of revenue through taxes and licence fees.

In a further evolution of coffee-drinking culture, cappuccino coffee was inspired by an Italian priest from the Capuchin monastic order who had fought against the Turks besieging Vienna in 1683. He acquired some of the coffee beans captured from the Ottoman spoils and began experimenting. Finding it too strong for his taste, he mixed it with cream and honey, which gave it the same colour brown as the Capuchins' robes and lent it a smoother taste. The Viennese named it *Kapuziner* in honour of the Capuchins, hence the Italian *cappuccino*, though the drink became popular in Italy only in the 1930s.

In Ivo Andrić's *Bridge over the Drina*, the *kapia* – a favoured outdoor meeting place – is located at the centre of the famous Ottoman bridge. It is the spot where the coffee-maker works, 'with his copper vessels and Turkish cups and ever-lighted charcoal brazier, and an apprentice who took the coffee over the way to the guests on the sofa' (i.e. the stone bench with the bridge parapet as its back).[8] Andrić also describes drinking *salep* and eating hot rolls on the bridge in winter.

Ayran and salep

The nomadic Ottomans brought with them from the steppes of Central Asia a salty, frothy yogurt drink called *ayran*, made from sheeps' milk and still drunk chilled in Turkey and the Balkans as a reviver or refresher. To combat winter cold they later devised a hot white milky drink called *salep*, thickened with dried wild Anatolian orchid root mixed with rosewater and sugar. Both these drinks are natural, unprocessed foods, perfect if you are on the move, with no time to sit down and eat a proper meal.

Boza (millet beer)

Ottomans used magnificent Iznik ceramic tankards to drink a kind of fermented millet called *boza*. Fermented cereal drinks have been produced and drunk in Anatolia and Mesopotamia since the 9th millennium bce, as excavations at Turkey's oldest archaeological site, the temple sanctuary at Göbeklitepe, near today's Gaziantep, have shown. Beer became popular in the 10th century CE among Central Asian Turkic peoples, becoming a common trade in towns and cities under the Ottomans and across the Balkans. Surprisingly, *boza* was banned by the heavy-drinking Selim II, nicknamed 'the Sot' (r. 1566–74), after a variation known as *Tartar boza*, frequently laced with opium, was produced. As with coffee and smoking, the prohibition would be reinforced then loosened several times over the course of the empire's history. Evliya Çelebi reports that *boza* was widely drunk in his day (the 17th century), when 300 *boza* shops employed over 1,000 people in Istanbul alone. Serbia, Montenegro, Bosnia and Herzegovina, Kosovo, Bulgaria, Albania and North Macedonia still produce *boza* today. Mevlut Karataş, the main character in Orhan Pamuk's 2014 novel *A Strangeness in my Mind* (*Kafamda Bir Tuhaflık*), is a *boza* vendor.

Boza contained only 1 per cent alcohol and was widely drunk by the janissaries. As Evliya Çelebi noted, there were numerous *boza*-makers in the army; he adds that 'to drink sufficient *boza* to cause intoxication is sinful but, unlike wine, in small quantities it is not condemned'.[9]

In 1876, the two brothers Hacı Ibrahim and Hacı Sadik established a *boza* shop in the Istanbul district of Vefa. Their *boza*, with its thick consistency and tart flavour, became famous throughout the city. It is the only *boza* shop dating from that period still in business, and is now run by the founders' great-great-grandchildren.

Wine and rakı

Throughout the Ottoman Empire wine was made by the Greeks and the Armenians, though its consumption was not confined to Christians. Many of the sultans were known to drink wine and *rakı*, often to excess, as with Selim the Sot, and attempts were made to ban it periodically, in the same way as coffee and smoking. When Süleyman the Magnificent imposed a ban in 1562, he even legislated that drunks were to be punished by having molten lead poured down their throats. The prohibitions never lasted long, however. The Habsburg Austrian ambassador Ogier Ghiselin de Busbecq pleaded that the 1562 ban be rescinded, claiming that if his retinue were denied wine they would fall sick and perhaps die. Şani, a contemporary Turkish poet, likewise expressed his feelings on the ban: 'The jars are broken, the goblet is empty, wine is no more/We are enslaved to coffee, oh what times these are.'[10]

In the early centuries of Ottoman rule there were no alcohol taxes since, strictly speaking, Islamic law forbade the consumption of alcohol. Ever pragmatic, however, the Ottomans introduced a tax on alcohol in the 17th century, known as the *müskiratresmi*, which fluctuated between 10 and 20 per cent, though the wine used by Christian priests and monks for the mass was exempt, as was that destined for their own consumption. In the 19th century drinking houses were referred to euphemistically as 'sherbet houses'. Towards the very end of the empire, further tax changes favoured beer production over that of wine or *rakı*.

The history of *rakı* as we know it today, the strong aniseed-flavoured spirit usually mixed with water, dates back to the 16th-century Ottoman era. According to Evliya Çelebi, there were several types of *rakı* produced by non-Muslims, often Armenians, in Istanbul, such as wine *rakı*, pomegranate *rakı*, anise *rakı*, date *rakı*, and even clover *rakı*. He wrote that its manufacture in Istanbul was prohibited, so the Armenians who produced the spirit based themselves in Çorlu, a town outside Istanbul on the road to Edirne, from where it was transported to the capital, especially to the taverns of Galata and Kasımpaşa.

Today *rakı* is widely considered to be Turkey's national alcoholic beverage, even though President Erdoğan, a non-alcohol-drinking Muslim, claims it should be *ayran*.

Pekmez

Pekmez is a syrup made from boiled fruit, usually grapes, mulberry, rosehip or pomegranate. Introduced by the Oghuz Turks, it was drunk to build up strength after injury and is reputed to be especially efficacious in those who have lost a lot of blood or suffer from iron deficiency. In the Balkans, it is more jam-like in texture and usually made of plums, whereas in Greece it is called *petimezi*. In Arab cuisine it can be made from dates or carob and is used for the same purposes, as a reviver and strength-builder during convalescence.

Viennese cafes and chocolate recipes

Viennese coffee shops claim to have a unique atmosphere, yet to anyone familiar with Turkey and the Arab world they feel very typical in that their customers can linger as long as they like, chatting, playing games or just reading the newspaper by themselves. The coffee is also served with a glass of water, exactly as in Turkey and the former Ottoman provinces, and replenished without the need to ask, even if no more coffee is ordered. This is referred to as *Wiener Art* (German for 'the Viennese way'), which erases any hint of its Ottoman past.

A very special chocolate recipe, a mix of Turkish coffee and Swiss absinthe, was invented by Tatari Oğuz Effendi (1831–1871). This eccentric Ottoman art connoisseur was said to have sealed his secret recipe in a bottle and tossed it into the Rhine at Basel in 1861, an event that Basel City Council chose to commemorate 150 years later with a plaque on its Middle Rhine Bridge in 2011. Today the exclusive product is sold by the Basel-based Beschle Chocolatier Suisse in single truffle packages and called 'The Lore of Tatari Oğuz Effendi'.

On a more mundane level, in 1914, before the outbreak of the First World War and the demise of the Ottoman Empire, the English chocolate company Fry's launched Turkish Delight, a pink, rose-flavoured lokum covered in milk chocolate. Its advertising slogan of the late 1950s, 'Full of Eastern Promise', was accompanied in early television adverts with a memorable jingle and a luscious belly dancer flashing her eyes seductively at the camera. It became part of the consciousness of every British child of the 1960s, and played a role in confirming an image of harems and seduction that already dominated Western minds.

10 Patriarch Georgios Kourtesios Scholarios takes the patent/warrant and imperial decrees of religious freedom from Sultan Mehmet II. Painting of the wall mosaic at the Constantinople Patriarchate Church of Ayias Yedriyias.

11 Istanbul Observatory, 1575, one of the largest in the world at the time. The two-way traffic of scientific exchanges between Western Europe and the Ottoman Empire has long been underestimated. Miniature from the Topkapı collection, 1575.

2 Installation of an armillary globe, experiment on the earth's gravity. Groups of highly skilled scientists were involved in developing instruments of this kind. Taqi al-Din (1526–1585), for example, collaborated with a Jewish mathematician from Thessalonica known as Davud the Mathematician. Page from a 16th-century Ottoman astronomical treatise.

13 An illuminated frontispiece of a collection of poems by Rumi (Mevlana),
Masnavi i Ma'navi, written in Persian, dated to 1461.

14 LEFT: Female musician playing a *çeng*, an Ottoman harp traditionally played by women, popular till the late 17th century. It is undergoing something of a revival in Turkey in recent years.

15 RIGHT: Woman playing a lute. Documentation from the 16th century shows that musical ensembles in the palace during the reign of Süleyman the Magnificent often included women.

16 Greek-language Ottoman café music remained popular as far afield as Egypt and the USA well after the dissolution of the Ottoman Empire, as illustrated by this photo of a Greek band and singer at the Port Said Café, W.29th St, New York, taken in 1959.

17 Preparation of remedies for smallpox under the instruction of Avicenna, from a 17th-century Ottoman manuscript called the *Treaty of Medicine* after physician and philosopher Avicenna (Ibn Sina), 990–1037.

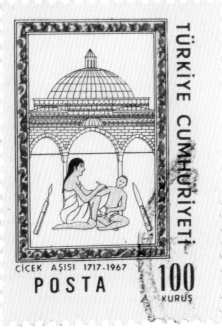

18 A Turkish stamp issued in 1967 commemorating 250 years since the practice of smallpox vaccination was first adopted in Ottoman Istanbul in 1717, many years before Edward Jenner (1749–1823) introduced it to England. The sultan issued a decree for mandatory vaccination in 1840, and the unvaccinated were fined and banned from school and employment.

9 Turkish carpets, much stronger than Persian carpets thanks to their symmetrical hard-wearing double knot, known as the Turkish knot, were much coveted in Europe as high-status possessions. They were often used to decorate walls and tables, as illustrated here in the painting of Georg Gisze by German artist Hans Holbein the Younger (*c.* 1497–1543).

20 Mehmet II's own complex, known as the Fatih (meaning 'Conqueror'), was built from 1463 to 1470, and explicitly set out to rival the Byzantine Hagia Sophia. Its distinctive identity helped project the political authority and power of the court and confirm Mehmet's status as leader of a world empire that straddled both Asia and Europe.

21 Bread was a staple of the Ottoman diet. Anonymous hand-coloured photograph, *c*. 1890–1900, entitled *Cook on a street in Constantinople.*

12
Home and Lifestyle

GRAND IMPERIAL BUILDING projects such as mosques and palaces give insights into the public face of the Ottomans, but there is also much that they have bequeathed in the private, domestic sphere.

The Ottoman house

One remarkable legacy is a type of house that developed in western Anatolia from the early 1300s and remains in use today, often converted into a boutique hotel for tourists. It evolved in regions where the Turks were dominant and has come to be known as the 'Turkish *hayat* house', in which the Arabic word *hayat* ('life') has the dual meaning of both 'open living' and 'open gallery'.[1] The design, based on a covered internal gallery that runs round three sides of the dwelling, has the effect of opening up and joining the various parts of the house so that it forms the perfect environment for a functioning family unit. The everyday activities of the household – cooking, baking bread, sewing, washing, drying fruit and cutting firewood – most of which were carried out by women, required such ample, flexible space. On the ground floor there were typically large storage areas and stables for a donkey, mule or horses, chicken coops in the courtyard, and a garden. The well, fountain and lavatories were also at ground level. These working spaces of the house were planned to open onto the courtyard and were closed off to the street (there were no windows), to allow for privacy and to prolong the life of produce kept in the storerooms. On the main living floor above, rooms gave onto the wooden gallery overlooking the courtyard and also, from the 17th century onwards, burst out towards the street in the form of bold overhangs, through whose latticed windows the family, and especially the women, could observe the outside world in the street below.

For all these reasons, the *hayat* house embodied the socio-cultural world of its Ottoman inhabitants. They never gave up their gardens. The house also mimicked, as much as possible, the natural environment that the Turks always preferred, even once they had become a settled population. In old imperial censuses, the nomad population is referred to as the *göçerev*, or the 'migrating house'. Semantically, the tent and the house corresponded to the family. Even nowadays, the tradition of leaving cities in the summer months in favour of high mountains and plateaux (or maybe the coast) lives on as an almost ritual migration. Today, *hayat* houses can still be found all over the former Ottoman provinces, built from a mix of stone, mud brick and timber, a wonderful legacy of a lost lifestyle. In keeping with the Ottoman preference for heights, they are almost always built on hillsides and take full advantage of the natural topography of the land, partly because this gave each house more privacy, a view and allowed cooling air to circulate, but also because it ensured natural drainage in times of heavy rainfall.

Turkey probably retains the most perfect examples of Ottoman residential architecture, in the town of Safranbolu, near the Black Sea coast, placed on UNESCO's World Heritage List in 1994. It is described as being 'a typical Ottoman city', one whose layout demonstrates organic growth in response to economic expansion.[2] The UNESCO entry goes on to mention how the main rooms on the first floors of these houses are usually wood-panelled, often with lavishly carved and painted ceilings, as well as built-in cupboards, fireplaces, shelves and benches. The rooms are multi-functional and are connected via halls called *sofa*, which, like the open wooden galleries, are very important elements of the house. In terms of function, this arrangement has echoes of the interconnecting rooms of Turkic tents, and the storage of clothing, utensils and bedding in woven bags hung from their side walls.

In the Balkans, examples of the Turkish *hayat* house can still be found across North Macedonia and in its capital, Skopje, and in cities such as Plovdiv in Bulgaria. In Albania, there are two former Ottoman towns, Berat and Gjirokastër, which are so well preserved that they too were inscribed on the UNESCO World Heritage List, in 2005 and 2008 respectively, in belated recognition of their importance. The UNESCO entry makes the point that such houses were not solely lived in by Muslims, but also bear witness to a way of life that 'has respected Orthodox Christian traditions which have thus been able to continue their spiritual and cultural development, particularly at Berat'.[3] The large Christian minority, in other words, peacefully coexisted with the Muslim majority. The houses date mainly from the 17th, 18th and 19th centuries and were lived in by craftsmen and merchants. The UNESCO entry continues: 'Berat and Gjirokastra bear outstanding testimony to the diversity of urban societies in the Balkans, and to longstanding ways of life which have today almost vanished.'

The Arab provinces

The Old City of Damascus boasts the last great concentration of Ottoman residential architecture anywhere in the world, with the Ottoman Yearbook[4] of 1900 listing 16,832 houses in the Old City, around half of which are still standing today. Aleppo, too, still has some courtyard houses, though not as many as Damascus, whereas Cairo, Jerusalem and Istanbul have lost most of theirs. In Damascus much of the urban fabric is either in the process of rapid change or under threat from development or neglect.

Cairo retains surprisingly little of its historical residential architecture because so much was destroyed by unenlightened urban planners. Just a handful of grand houses remain, built for wealthy merchants or officials, but the same defining Ottoman design principles are clear, namely the need to achieve privacy for the family unit, especially the women, and to give protection from the climate. Urban houses for the wealthy could have up to three separate courtyards. The entrance corridor from the street featured a right-angled bend so that there was never a direct view from the street, even into the first courtyard, which was the reception area for male guests (Ottoman Turkish *selamlik*). Behind that, at a further remove from the street, was the courtyard for the women and children (Ottoman Turkish *haramlık*), which always had the greatest concentration of beautiful decor and carving. Upper-floor windows to the street had perforated wooden screens called *mashrabiyya*. A third, smaller, more functional courtyard was where the servants lived and did the cooking (Ottoman Turkish *khadamlık*).

What is known today as the Gayer-Anderson Museum occupies one such house in Cairo – in fact two houses, joined by a bridge at an upper floor level, built into the outer wall of the Ibn Tulun Mosque in the 1630s. There used to be many houses built up against mosque walls for support, but this one, known locally as the *Bait al-Kritliyya* (the 'House of the Cretan Woman', after its wealthy Ottoman Muslim owner from Crete), is the only one to have survived the urban planning disasters of the 1920s. Gayer-Anderson himself, a retired major, lived there only from 1935 to 1942 before returning to England, but bequeathed it to the Egyptian government, in return for which King Farouq awarded him the title of Pasha. Its reception room, galleried loggia with *mashrabbiya* wooden latticework and roof terrace were the setting for an early scene in the 1977 James Bond film *The Spy Who Loved Me*.

Lifestyle

The tent

The sheer centrality of the tent to the Ottoman way of life is hard to overstate. When Europeans first saw the interiors of Ottoman tents they were astonished at their scale, their colours and their 'exoticism'. Ambassadors from Austria visited Süleyman the Magnificent in his imperial tent and described themselves as 'speechless corpses' at the sight of the rich festoons of colourful appliqué and gilded leather. They were status symbols designed to impress, but also on occasion took on an almost mystical quality. In the preface to the Album of Sultan Ahmet Khan,[5] the author, an Ottoman subject addressing his sultan, writes:

> May the respected tents of my sovereign as mighty as Jamshed [a mythological Persian king], refuge of the world, be extended and stretched with the eternal pegs and ropes of his generous, felicitous being.[6]

Ottoman tents were mobile palaces, so elaborate that they required a dedicated official – the head tent-setter – to manage them. In their second capital at Edirne, the Ottomans, who used tents both as military encampments and as homes, still maintained semi-permanent encampments on the outskirts of the city 'as an integral part of its built and urban landscape, an extension in felt, leather, and weaving to the stone, mortar, and wood of the city's mosques, markets, and dwellings.'[7]

As we have seen, many art historians have suggested that the Topkapı Palace was designed as a kind of stationary tent complex (see pp. 159–60). Even in their early nomadic lives, the Turkic tribes had many different types of tent, such as the bathroom tent, the kitchen tent, the prisoner tent, and even the ominous execution tent.

On the occasion of the circumcision of Ahmet III's sons in 1720, there was a 15-day festival based in a tent city specially erected on the Bosphorus, where 10,000 jars of sherbet were ordered for the guests. The sultan commissioned a special book to commemorate the event, which described the banqueting tent, the gunners' tent, a tent replica of the Tower of Justice in the Topkapı Palace, and the imperial tent enclosed with a crenellated cloth fence so that it resembled a fortification.[8]

Many Ottoman tents have survived in European museums, although the finest collection can be seen in Istanbul's Military Museum in the Harbiye district. When the Ottomans were conquering new lands and expanding the empire, their tent culture was of crucial importance. The large army had to travel long distances and relied on a highly efficient organization, for which the experience and traditions of Turkish nomadic culture proved invaluable, especially the highly detailed advance preparations that they had honed from centuries of migration. The sultan's 'walled' tent palace was so large, according to the French traveller Antoine Galland, writing in 1673, that 600 camels were needed to carry the various parts; what is more, there were always two, so that one could be set up ahead while the other was being dismantled. The many surviving Ottoman miniature paintings give us insights into the ceremonial tents and their almost theatrical splendour. Their walls were often designed to look like pavilions, with magnificent embroidery in silk, silver and gold thread recreating the impression of panels of floral-patterned tiles.

European rulers including the French king Louis XIV were great admirers of the Ottoman tent, and a craze took hold in the 17th century whereby many tents à la Turque were used as venues for grand, fashionable parties. The two most famous Turkish tents in England were the one built in the gardens of Painshill, Surrey, owned by the Honourable Charles Hamilton, and that in Stourhead, Wiltshire, owned by Henry Colt Hoare; both appeared c. 1750. The Empress Josephine had a tent room at Malmaison; and the third Marquess of Hertford, nicknamed the 'Caliph of Regent's Park', had a tent room made for him by Decimus Burton at St Dunstan's Villa that sadly burnt down in 1930.

The Turkish word köşk (our word 'kiosk') is a natural extension of the tent culture, evolving gradually into a kind of garden pavilion in which coffee and beverages were served, like modern conservatories. Simpler versions of the kiosk decorate many European gardens and parks in the form of bandstands or distinctive tourist information booths.

The 'Ottoman' couch

The key piece of furniture in the Ottoman home was a padded, upholstered seat or bench, without arms or a back, that in most Western languages is still known as an 'ottoman'. Highly versatile, it was traditionally heaped with cushions and could be placed up against a wall or in the centre of a room; it could vary in size from a full-length bed for reclining on, to a square, circular or octagonal seat that could be moved about according to where it was needed or even just used as a footrest. It was introduced into the West from Istanbul in the late 18th century, making its way into every fashionable boudoir, and during the 19th century it became a prominent feature in gentlemen's clubs, where it was sometimes divided into separate seating spaces by arms, given a central padded column to lean against and provided with a hinged seat for storage. Again, its defining feature was its flexibility, another legacy of the Ottoman nomadic tent culture in which such furnishings as existed had to be multi-purpose and adaptable, never fixed.

Clothing

KAFTANS

The Ottomans used luxurious silk textiles for furnishings and for clothing, many of which have influenced European styles across the centuries. The most prestigious were velvet and complex silk weaves, often incorporating thread wrapped with silver or gilded silver. Bursa in north-west Anatolia was the main centre for silk-weaving, an industry established in the 15th century largely to compete with Italian imports. Velvet brocade, or *çatma*, was used for clothing as well as furnishings such as cushion covers and featured carnation or rosebud patterns in bright motifs of metal-wrapped thread set against the silk velvet background. Elaborately embroidered brocaded waistcoats worn by both Ottoman men and women became ladies' high fashion items in Europe, as did kaftans, which were worn by high-ranking Ottoman men, but in Europe mainly by women. Queen Victoria's granddaughter Alix of Hesse wore a loose-fitting kaftan at her coronation in 1896, in stark contrast to the tight-fitting corseted dresses common in England in the 1890s, and the kaftan gradually grew in popularity, with fashion designers including Christian Dior including it as a loose evening gown in their collections by the 1950s. Often colourfully patterned in bold colours, kaftans became especially popular in the late 1960s and 1970s as part of the 'hippie trail' culture and as gowns for at-home casual entertaining. Elizabeth Taylor wore a designer kaftan at her second wedding to Richard Burton in 1975.

HAREM PANTS

Harem pants were direct copies of the Ottoman şalvar: loose-fitting trousers taken in at the ankle worn by both men and women in the Ottoman Empire, irrespective of rank or social standing. Again, like the kaftan, their comfort was a key selling point, and in 1911 the Paris couturier Paul Poiret added harem pants to his collection, calling them his 'Style Sultane' and marketing them as liberating to European women, who had not worn trousers of any description up till then. He used the imagery of sultans and the harem to highlight the Orientalizing style as exotic, sometimes calling them 'sultan skirts'.

THE FEZ

This distinctive Ottoman hat, made of felt, was dyed using a crimson berry from the Moroccan city of Fez, hence its name. Mahmud II (r. 1808–39) ordered the wearing of the fez rather than the traditional turban as a modernizing measure: it would allow men to prostrate themselves fully and press their heads to the floor while praying. In 1827, 50,000 fezzes were ordered from Tunis for the sultan's troops, and the head-wear was also made compulsory for civil servants in 1829 as a part of his egalitarian reform. The fez became a symbol of modernity throughout the empire, worn by Muslims, Christians and Jews alike. It was used by Christians and Muslims in the Balkans throughout the 19th and 20th centuries, though in semi-independent Montenegro Orthodox citizens wore their fezzes with a Greek cross on front, while those of the South Slavs in Croatia featured a star and crescent, and in 1850 the red fezzes of the Serbians displayed the Serbian coat of arms.

Atatürk banned the fez in Turkey in 1925 as part of his own modernizing reforms, but it remained popular in the West as part of men's luxury smoking outfits and in gentlemen's clubs. In Morocco it is still widely worn, especially by members of the royal court, and was considered a symbol of resistance against French colonial rule.

Towels

The invention of towels is usually associated with 17th-century Bursa, where strips of cloth called *pestamel* were employed in Turkish baths because they were absorbent. By the 18th century these towels began to feature protruding loops of thread that formed a pile; these looped towels became known as *havly*, meaning 'with loops', which changed over time to *havlu*, Turkish for 'towel'. Towels became widely affordable in the West only in the 19th century with the cotton trade and industrialization. The Lancashire-based company of Christy & Sons, founded in 1850, was the first to industrialize the production of looped-cotton 'terrycloth' towels, originally known as 'the Turkish towel', after Christy's son spotted examples in an Istanbul market. Queen Victoria was an early fan after seeing them at the 1851 Great Exhibition.

Jewelry

The Ottoman Empire was highly regarded for the quality of its gold- and silverwork, crafted mainly by Armenians and Jews. Items of jewelry were given as dowries and gifts, and often incorporated Persian and Byzantine motifs, with the designs of Constantinople influencing metalwork across the empire. Watchmaking was a particular Ottoman interest, as a result of which many European goldsmiths and watchmakers moved to Constantinople, where they worked in the foreigners' quarter around the Galata Tower known as Pera (today's Beyoğlu).

Tulips and tulip mania

The Seljuks are thought to have been responsible for the introduction of the tulip bulb into Anatolia from Central Asia, where the flowers grew wild in the valleys of the Heavenly Mountain on the China–Kazakhstan border. The tulip is not mentioned by any writer in antiquity. The first known illustration of a tulip is on a tile in the palace of the Seljuk ruler Alaeddin Keykubad bin Keykavus (r. 1220–37), and by the 15th century the flower had come to be regarded as the symbol of the Ottomans. Mehmet the Conqueror ordered tulips to be planted in the new parks and gardens he created in Constantinople after the conquest. Himself a keen gardener, he is known to have enjoyed working the terraces and flowerbeds of the Topkapı Palace for relaxation. Süleyman the Magnificent also promoted the tulip tradition, encouraging their planting and using tulip imagery in his poems. In Istanbul, the relatively peaceful 'Tulip Period' (1718–30) was a time when-the Ottoman Empire began to orient itself towards Europe; art and architecture became more elaborate and 'florid' under the influence of the European Baroque style, as exemplified in the Fountain of Ahmet III (1728) in front of the Topkapı Palace.

Western diplomats such as Ogier Ghiselin de Busbecq, ambassador of the Austrian Habsburgs to the court of Süley-man the Magnificent, observed the flower in 1554 and sent consignments back to Austria. The tulip craze spread rapidly across Europe, and in France in the early 17th century entire properties were exchanged as payment for a single rare tulip bulb. During the speculative frenzy now known as 'tulip mania', the bulbs became so expensive that they were treated as a form of currency, like speculative futures in today's stock markets, and the flower was frequently depicted in Dutch Golden Age paintings. The Dutch government was forced to introduce trading restrictions in 1634, which led to the collapse of the market three years later. It is generally thought to represent the first recorded bursting of an asset bubble in history. The term 'tulip mania' has even entered the English language, used metaphorically to refer to any large economic bubble in which prices outstrip an item's intrinsic value.

In Iran, the tulip is the national symbol for martyrdom and has featured on stamps and coins. It was commonly used in the 1979 Islamic Revolution and appeared on the Iranian flag. In modern Turkey it is still considered the embodiment of per-fection and beauty. It appears as a discreet grey emblem on the fuselage of Turkish Airlines aircraft. The word for tulip in both Persian and Turkish is *lâle*, often used as a girl's name. When written in Arabic script, *lâle* has the same letters as 'Allah', which is why the flower also became a holy symbol, widely associated with the House of Osman, the founder of the Ottoman dynasty, and commonly used as a decorative motif on tiles, fabrics and ceramics of all kinds.

As for the flower itself, fourteen different species of tulip can be found in Turkey today, mainly in red, yellow, white and variegated mutations, while breeding programmes have produced thousands of hybrids. The Netherlands remains the world's largest tulip producer, and tulip festivals are held all round the world, as far afield as Canada, the United States and Australia.

CONCLUSION
Lessons for the Future?

DID PEOPLE LIVE happily ever after, I found myself wondering, once they were 'freed from the Ottoman yoke'? Across the three continents the Ottoman Empire once straddled, I struggled to think of a place where this might be the case. The Arab provinces were carved into unnatural entities for the Allies' convenience after the First World War and have suffered ever since. The Ottoman provinces of historic Syria, which at one time stretched right down to the Sinai Peninsula, are today the powder-keg mix of Israel, the Occupied Palestinian Territory, Lebanon, Jordan and Syria. Ottoman tributary states in Eastern Europe like Podalia (part of modern Ukraine), Moldavia, Wallachia, Transylvania and the Crimean Khanate fell victim to complex wars initiated by the Russian imperial agenda, eerily echoing the current Russian invasion of Ukraine. The Balkan countries, once 'liberated', proceeded to turn on themselves in the name of nationalism, becoming 'a panoply of small, unviable, mutually antagonistic and internally intolerant states';[1] it was a disaster that resulted in some of the worst massacres in European history, giving us the very word 'balkanization'. Bosnians today fear pro-Russian actors will use the Ukraine crisis to stir up big trouble in the Balkans.

The long road trip from England to Albania I completed in October 2021 involved crossing twenty national borders. Each set of officials – and each set of entry rules for the COVID-19 pandemic – served to reinforce the message that borders accentuate differences, a fact that frequently leads to divisive disputes. Juggling between separate currencies and languages, sometimes three in one day, left me with a sense of the political fragility across the region, where communities are moving ever further apart, no longer even learning each other's languages. When Serbian officials refused me entry to Kosovo, saying it was 'too dangerous' and forcing me to find an entry point via Montenegro instead, it reminded me of a similar experience with Israeli border guards in 2016 who declined to let me into the Occupied Palestinian Territory for the same reason; I had to travel a further 50 kilometres (30 miles) to a different crossing. No such 'danger' existed in either case, but the barrier was erected to perpetuate the political separation of communities.

The concept of 'the Balkans' did not even exist under the Ottomans. The term, derived from the name of the main mountain range in the peninsula, was not popularized until Western travellers, journalists and propagandists started flocking to the area before the outbreak of the First Balkan War in 1912. Before that, the Ottomans themselves simply called the area 'Rumeli', meaning 'of Rome', since these lands had formerly belonged to Rome and were acquired from Byzantium centuries earlier. European scholars well into the 19th century generally used the phrase 'European Turkey' to denote the region and considered all Orthodox Christians there to be Greeks, with little understanding of the separate Slavonic population.[2] European knowledge of 'Turkish' geography was vague and maps imperfect until, between 1878 and 1908, a series of Great

Power diplomatic conferences began carving up Ottoman territory into a succession of nationalist states, a process of disintegration that has continued into the 21st century. Could history be at risk of repeating itself, threatening the EU project? States such as Montenegro and Kosovo have already broken away from Serbia, in 2006 and 2008 respectively, while countries such as Crimea in 2014 and Ukraine in 2022 have been the target of President Vladimir Putin's renewed Russian expansionism.

The case of Crete provides one example of the games that can be played with political concepts of national sovereignty. After the Ottomans had captured most of the island from the Venetians in 1647 they restored the rights enjoyed by the local Orthodox Church, formerly suppressed by the Catholic Venetians. A quarter of the original Orthodox population converted to Islam, viewing the Ottomans as liberators from Catholic repression. Greek independence then led to their persecution as Muslims, so they chose to seek refuge under Ottoman provincial rule, many fleeing to Syria, where there are communities of Cretan Muslims to this day. Coming full circle, some have now returned to Crete as refugees, fleeing the ongoing Syrian war.[3]

In another example, when Osman of Timişoara, an Ottoman Muslim from today's Romania, was captured in the chaos that followed the failed siege of Vienna in 1683, he was forced by his Habsburg masters to work as a slave for twelve years, enduring many humiliations before escaping over the border back to Ottoman lands. Within his lifetime he saw his hometown of Timişoara, where he had lived alongside Orthodox and Jewish communities, fall to the Austrian army. The Muslim population was expelled, and it was then colonized by German Catholics, before the Orthodox Church eventually reasserted itself.[4] Ironically, Osman returned to Vienna towards the end of his life

in 1726, as diplomatic translator for the first permanent Ottoman consul in the city. His memoir, written over 300 years
ago as a deep meditation on the dilemmas of identity, difference and belonging, rings as true today as it did then.[5]

Nostalgia for the days of empire still exists in the countries
of the former Austro-Hungarian and Russian territories to this
day, just as it does in Turkey. Yet the notion of a golden age of
sultans who fostered ethnic and religious coexistence is just
as misleading as the intensely nationalistic prisms that continue to lay the blame for the sectarian violence that plagues
the Balkans and the Middle East today firmly at the door
of the Ottomans. True religious coexistence was more the norm
under Ottoman rule than anywhere in Christendom before the
late 17th century, but it would be false to claim that it represented a utopian equality between religions. Islam's superiority
was built into the system from the start, making it economically
attractive to convert in order to pay less tax. Likewise, the relative lack of ethnic conflict cannot be attributed to some kind of
advanced sense of tolerance of 'the other' but, rather, reflected
the absence of any concept of nationality across the empire.
People thought of themselves as Ottomans, not as Romanians,
Egyptians or Turks. When the Albanian commander Muhammad Ali broke away from his Ottoman masters in Istanbul
to found his own dynasty in Cairo in 1805, he still thought of
himself as an Ottoman and endowed his home town of Kavala
in Macedonia with an Ottoman-style *külliye*.

In some ways, perhaps, it was the Turks whose nationalist sentiments won the day, under their charismatic leader,
Mustafa Kemal, later known as Atatürk, 'Father of the Turks'.
Under Atatürk, everyone in the modern Turkish republic, set up
in 1923, was now required be a 'Turk'. His breed of nationalism

represented the opposite of the Ottoman approach, whereby the Kurds, for example, had been simply Muslims, the same as Turks, Arabs and Persians. The Kurds were certainly among the losers after the First World War. The British and French reneged on their initial pledge to set up a separate state of Kurdistan, Atatürk reclassified them as 'mountain Turks', and their language and culture were suppressed, leading to the hostility and separatist movements that have dominated the relationship between the Kurds and the Turkish state ever since.

In today's Turkey, President Erdoğan and his AK party, in power for two decades, have been the architects of a neo-Ottoman nostalgia trip, promoting a vision in which the achievements of their Ottoman ancestors proved the superiority of the 700-year period when Islam was the official state religion. This, in their eyes, is Islam's rightful status, ripped from them by Atatürk's drastic reforms that closed dervish *tekkes*, abolished the caliphate and replaced Ottoman Turkish, written in the Arabic script, with modern Turkish, written using the Latin alphabet and purged of Arabic and Persian loan words.

To cement the new Ottoman vision into the public consciousness, the Turkish government embarked upon mega-projects such as the Grand Çamlıca Mosque in Üsküdar. Now the largest mosque in Turkey, it dominates the Asian skyline of the Bosphorus with its six minarets, a number previously reserved for the Grand Mosque in Mecca. Designed by two Turkish women architects working in the style of Sinan, it constitutes a conscious challenge to Sinan's Süleymaniye Mosque and its four minarets on the European side – even if, to confirm its 21st-century credentials, it also offers a museum, an art gallery and childcare facilities.

In Erdoğan's Turkey, anniversaries of the 1453 conquest of Istanbul are celebrated in grand style, and Ottoman themes appear on new banknotes. The Gezi Park riots in 2013 were triggered by Erdoğan's plans to turn the park into a giant shopping-mall replica of an Ottoman barracks. He was forced to backtrack in the face of strong opposition. Erdoğan named his controversial thousand-room palace in Ankara a *külliye*, following the Ottoman tradition of a complex centred on a mosque, but the project's extravagance and illegality (it is built within the Atatürk Forest Farm, where construction is forbidden) have confirmed the view of many that he sees himself as a latter-day sultan.

Are there lessons to be learnt from the Ottomans? Some will throw their hands up in horror at the very idea, but my own view, at the end of writing this book on their cultural legacy, is that much of their early success and subsequent longevity can be attributed to two inter-related elements. First, their readiness to foster talent from across their empire. Their mindset was anti-elitist: they did not favour people simply because of their high birth or their ethnicity, but filled their top political and strategic positions with those who showed themselves most capable. As a result, the empire was, on the whole, efficiently administered by people of real ability. Second, their openness towards refugees: the Ottomans took in displaced people of all religions and ethnicities, helped them get back on their feet, and then turned them into loyal tax-paying citizens. It is a legacy that lives on in the former Arab provinces, and indeed in Turkey itself, where it has shown itself most recently in the region's response to the displacement of more than half of modern Syria's population of 23 million.

Most European countries were cast into disarray by the arrival of just 1 million Syrian refugees in 2015/16, but the overwhelming

majority of asylum-seekers made their way to the neighbouring states of Lebanon, Jordan and Turkey, whose economies
have been placed under considerable strain as a result – even
if more than 90 per cent are not in UNHCR refugee camps but
have self-settled and are economically active. Before the current
crisis, the Syrians themselves had welcomed, in keeping with
the Ottoman tradition they had inherited, mass influxes of Pal-
estinians in the 1940s and 1960s following the creation of Israel;
Lebanese in the 1970s and 1980s during their own civil war; and
Iraqis fleeing their homeland following the US invasion of 2003.
It was simply a social and ethical norm, an instinctive reaction
by individuals and local communities, and not mandated by
any government decree. Maybe the current large-scale refugee
influx from Ukraine, fleeing the 2022 Russian invasion, will cata-
lyze a new and properly coordinated European migration policy,
in the same way that the huge refugee exodus from Circassia,
Abkhazia and Crimea, escaping Imperial Russia's aggressions,
led directly to the 1857 Ottoman Refugee Code.

All cultures borrow and rework elements from other cultures, but the Ottomans were unusually open on that front
too. They were happy to acknowledge their civilizational debt
to their Seljuk and Roman forbears while holding true to their
own tribal nomadic identity and also absorbing many new influences, especially from China, Iran, and the Arab and Byzantine
worlds. Tiles perhaps represent the most perfect embodiment
of this synthesis. An Ottoman tile is always immediately recognizable, just as is a Persian, Armenian or Palestinian tile. All
share certain similarities in colour, composition and motifs, but
the differences that make them distinctive are to do with their
particular colour combinations, their particular blend of motifs,
and the way the compositions are envisaged in the first place.

A Turkish tile has a certain boldness, a more architectural quality to its use of cypress trees, tulips, long stems and elongated *saz* leaves when compared, for instance, with Persian examples. The relationship between the different traditions, even as they remain visibly distinct, serves as a good metaphor for the Ottomans' attitude to other cultures. Each would not be the way it is, were it not for the influence of the others.

Where the Ottomans had a presence that lasted centuries, Ottoman urbanism is still clear to see. In Balkan cities such as Thessalonica, Sofia and Belgrade, there have all too often been wilful attempts to eradicate it, while in Middle Eastern cities, including Damascus and Cairo, the Ottoman landmarks sit more easily alongside those of earlier Islamic dynasties. Mosques remain in use and are very much part of the fabric of society. In a few other places – Sarajevo and Prizren, for example – the Ottoman city centres are still vibrant, with functioning mosques, churches and synagogues in close proximity. In the Balkans, many Ottoman bazaars and hammams have been repurposed into cultural centres or exhibition spaces, often in such a way as to obscure their 'alien' origins, yet it is ironic that Western tourists are still drawn by what they interpret as 'exotic', the very quality that local people reject as foreign to their national identity – never mind that their cuisine, popular culture and language remain clearly full of Turkish words and phrases.

In multi-ethnic and multi-religious cities all across the Ottoman Empire – from Izmir, Thessalonica and Jerusalem to Damascus, Aleppo and Istanbul itself – communities tended to self-segregate for residential purposes into their own religious groupings, but during the day there was constant and regular interaction in the markets and in shops that existed alongside each other, irrespective of religion or ethnicity. Fewer and fewer people are now alive who can remember how that coexistence worked and how it felt to live in such cities. A new generation of Turkish-speaking scholars is actively engaged in investigating that phenomenon, unearthing evidence from hitherto untapped voluminous Ottoman archives scattered across the empire's former provinces. The answers they come up with may even lead, another hundred years from now, to a total reassessment of the Ottoman cultural legacy.

SELECT BIBLIOGRAPHY

Aksoy, Bulent, 'Women in the Ottoman Musical Tradition',
 Osmanlı, vol. 10 (1999), pp. 788–813.

Almond, Ian, *Two Faiths, One Banner: When Muslims Marched
 with Christians across Europe's Battlegrounds* (London:
 I. B. Tauris, 2009).

Al-Rihawi, Abd Al-Qadir, and Emilie E. Ouechek, 'Les deux Takiyya
 de Damas: La Takiyya et la madrasa Sulaymaniyya du Marg et la
 Takiyya as-Salimiyya de Salih iyya', *Bulletin d'Études Orientales*,
 vol. 28 (1975), pp. 218–25.

Andrić, Ivo, *The Bridge over the Drina* [1945], trans. Lovett F. Edwards
 (London: Harvill, 1994).

Aslanapa, Oktay, *Turkish Art and Architecture*, trans. Adair Mill
 (London: Faber & Faber, 1971).

Asuero, Pablo Martín, *Descripción del Damasco Otomano (1807–1920)*
 (Madrid: Miraguano Ediciones, 2004).

Baer, Marc David, *The Ottomans: Khans, Caesars and Caliphs*
 (London: Basic Books, 2021).

Bakhit, Muhammad Adnan, *The Ottoman Province of Damascus
 in the Sixteenth Century* (Beirut: Librairie du Liban), 1982.

Ball, Warwick, *The Eurasian Steppe: People, Movement, Ideas*
 (Edinburgh: Edinburgh University Press, 2021).

——, *Sultans of Rome: The Turkish World Expansion* (London:
 East and West Publishing, 2012).

Barsoumian, Hagop, *The Eastern Question and the Tanzimat Era*
 (London: Macmillan, 1997).

Bloxham, Donald, *The Great Game of Genocide* (London: Oxford
 University Press, 2007).

Brotton, Jerry, *Trading Territories: Mapping the Early Modern World*
 (London: Reaktion, 2003).

Brown, L. Carl (ed.), *Imperial Legacy: The Ottoman Imprint on the
 Balkans and the Middle East* (New York: Columbia University
 Press, 1996).

Brummett, Palmira, *Mapping the Ottomans: Sovereignty, Territory and Identity in the Early Modern Mediterranean* (Cambridge: Cambridge University Press, 2015).

Bryer, Anthony, 'Greek historians on the Turks: The case of the first Byzantine-Ottoman marriage', in R. Davis and J. Wallace Hadrill (eds.), *The Writing of History in the Middle Ages* (Oxford: Oxford University Press, 1981).

Burns, Ross, *Damascus, A History* (London: Routledge, 2005).

Burton, Isabel, *The Inner Life of Syria, Palestine, and the Holy Land* (London: K. Paul, Trench & Co., 1884).

Çapağtay, Suna, *The First Capital of the Ottoman Empire: The Religious, Architectural and Social History of Bursa* (London: I. B. Tauris, 2020).

Casale, Giancarlo, *The Ottoman Age of Exploration* (New York and Oxford: Oxford University Press, 2010).

——(ed. and trans.), *Prisoner of the Infidels: The Memoir of an Ottoman Muslim in Seventeenth-Century Europe* (Berkeley: University of California Press, 2021).

Çelebi, Evliya, *Seyahatname*, 10 vols. (Istanbul, 1896–1938).

Chatty, Dawn, *Syria: The Making and Unmaking of a Refuge State* (London: Hurst, 2017).

Couroucli, Maria, and Tchavdar Marinov (eds.), *Balkan Heritages: Negotiating History and Culture*, British School at Athens – Modern Greek and Byzantine Studies, vol. 1 (Farnham: Ashgate, 2015).

Dankoff, Robert, and Sooyong Kim, *An Ottoman Traveller: Selections from the Book of Travels of Evliya Çelebi* (London: Eland, 2011).

Degeorge, Gérard, *Damascus* (Paris: Flammarion, 2004).

——and Yves Porter, *The Art of the Islamic Tile* (Paris: Flammarion, 2002).

Denny, Walter, *Provincial Ottoman Architecture and the Metropolitan Style, Questions of Meaning and Originality*, in F. Déroche (ed.), *Art Turc / Turkish Art: 10th International Congress of Turkish Art, Geneva 17–23 September 1995* (Geneva: Fondation Max van Berchem, 1999), pp. 243–52.

Ellis, Markman, *The Coffee House: A Cultural History* (London: Weidenfeld & Nicolson, 2011).

Engel, Carl, *Researches into the Early History of the Violin Family* (Amsterdam: Antiqua, 1965).

Erder, Leila T., 'The Making of Industrial Bursa', unpublished PhD thesis, Princeton University, 1976.

Erickson, Edward J., *Ottomans and Armenians: A Study in Counterinsurgency* (New York: Palgrave Macmillan, 2013).

Erzen, Yale, 'Sinan as Anti-Classicist', *Muqarnas*, no. 5 (1988), pp. 70–86.

Ettinghausen, Richard, and Oleg Grabar, *The Art and Architecture of Islam: 650–1250* (Harmondsworth: Penguin, 1987).

Faroqhi, Suraiya, 'The Business of Trade: Bursa Merchants of the 1480s', in Suraiya Faroqhi, *Making a Living in the Ottoman Lands* (Istanbul: The Isis Press, 1995), pp. 193–216.

——, *Travel and Artisans in the Ottoman Empire* (London: I. B. Tauris, 2014).

Farraj, Johnny, and Sami Abu Shumays, 'Introduction', *Inside Arabic Music* (New York: Oxford University Press, 2019).

Finkel, Caroline, *Osman's Dream: The Story of the Ottoman Empire, 1300–1923* (London: John Murray, 2005).

Frishman, Martin, and Hasan-Uddin Khan (eds.), *The Mosque: History, Architectural Development and Regional Diversity* (London: Thames & Hudson, 2002).

Gaunt, David, *The Assyrian Genocide of 1915* (2009), Assyrian Genocide Research Centre: www.seyfocenter.com/english/38/ (accessed 28 November 2021).

Gerber, Haim, 'Social and Economic Position of Women in an Ottoman City: Bursa, 1600–1700', *International Journal of Middle East Studies*, vol. 12, no. 3 (1980), pp. 231–44.

Goodwin, Godfrey, 'Sinan and City Planning', in 'Mimar Sinan. The Urban Vision', ed. Attilio Petroccioli, special issue of *Environmental Design*, vols. 5–6 (1987), pp. 10–19.

——, *Sinan: Ottoman Architecture and Its Values Today*, (London: Saqi, 2003).

Grabar, Oleg, *The Formation of Islamic Art* (New Haven, Conn., and London: Yale University Press, 1976).

Grabill, Joseph L., *Protestant Diplomacy and the Near East* (Minneapolis: University of Minnesota Press, 1971).

Greaves, John (ed.), *A Description of the Grand Signor's Seraglio, or the Turkish Emperor's Court* (London: Martin and Ridley, 1650).

Greble, Emily, *Muslims and the Making of Modern Europe* (Oxford: Oxford University Press, 2022).

Grehan, James, *Everyday Life and Consumer Culture in Eighteenth-Century Damascus* (Seattle: University of Washington Press, 2007).

Hamadeh, Shirine, *The City's Pleasures: Architectural Sensibility in Eighteenth-Century Istanbul* (Seattle: University of Washington Press, 2008).

Hanssen, Jens, Thomas Philipp and Stefan Weber (eds.), *The Empire in the City: Arab Provincial Capitals in the Late Ottoman Empire* (Beirut: Orient-Institut der DMG Beirut, 2002).

Havlioğlu, Didem, *Mihrî Hatun: Performance, Gender-Bending, and Subversion in Ottoman Intellectual History* (Syracuse, N.Y.: Syracuse University Press, 2017).

Hillenbrand, Carole, *Turkish Myth and Muslim Symbol: The Battle of Manzikert* (Edinburgh: Edinburgh University Press, 2007).

Hillenbrand, Robert, *Islamic Architecture. Form, Function and Meaning* (Edinburgh: Edinburgh University Press, 1994).

——, *Islamic Art and Architecture* (London: Thames & Hudson, 1999).

Hobsbawm, Eric J., *The Age of Revolution: Europe 1789–1848* (London: Weidenfeld & Nicolson, 1962).

Humphreys, R. Stephen, *Between Memory and Desire: T he Middle East in a Troubled Age* (Berkeley: University of California Press, 1999).

Hussain, Tharik, *Minarets in the Mountains* (Chesham: Bradt Guides, 2021).

Imber, Colin, 'The legend of Osman Gazi', in Colin Imber (ed.), *Studies in Ottoman History and Law* (Istanbul: Isis Press, 1996), pp. 323–31.

——, *The Ottoman Empire 1300–1650: The Structure of Power* (London: Red Globe Press, 3rd edn 2019).

Inalcık, Halil, and Donald Quataert (eds.), *An Economic and Social History of the Ottoman Empire, 1300–1919* (Cambridge: Cambridge University Press, 1994).

Kafescioğlu, Çiğdem, '"In the Image of Rum": Ottoman Architectural Patronage in Sixteenth-Century Aleppo and Damascus', *Muqarnas*, vol. 16 (1999), pp. 70–96.

Keenan, Brigid, *Damascus: Hidden Treasures of the Old City* (London: Thames & Hudson, 2000).

Kinross, Patrick, *The Ottoman Centuries: The Rise and Fall of the Turkish Empire* (New York: Morrow, 1977).

Kritzeck, James (ed.), *Anthology of Islamic Literature* (Harmondsworth: Penguin, 1964).

Kuban, Doğan, *The Miracle of Divriği* (Istanbul: YKY, 2001).

——, *Ottoman Architecture* (Woodbridge: Antique Collectors Club, 2010).

——, *The Turkish Hayat House* (Istanbul: Eren, 1995).

Kuran, Aptullah, 'Ottoman Classical Mosques in Istanbul and its Provinces', in *Theories and Principles of Design in the Architecture of Islamic Societies* (Cambridge, Mass.: The Aga Khan Program for Islamic Architecture, 1988), pp. 13–22.

Lepsius, Johannes, *Armenia and Europe: An Indictment*, ed. and trans. J. R. Harris (London: Hodder & Stoughton, 1897).

Levey, Michael, *The World of Ottoman Art* (London: Thames & Hudson, 1975).

Lewis, Bernard, *Istanbul and the Civilization of the Ottoman Empire* (Norman, Okla.: University of Oklahoma Press, 1963).

Lindner, Rudi, *Nomads and Ottomans in Medieval Anatolia* (Bloomington, Ind.: Indiana University, 1983).

Lowry, Heath, 'Pushing the stone uphill: The impact of bubonic plague on Ottoman urban society in the fifteenth and sixteenth centuries', *Journal of Ottoman Studies*, vol. 23 (2004), pp. 93–132.

——, *The Shaping of the Ottoman Balkans, 1350–1550: The Conquest, Settlement and Infrastructural Development of Northern Greece* (Istanbul: Bahçeşehir University Publications, 2008).

McCarthy, Justin, *Death and Exile: The Ethnic Cleansing of Ottoman Muslims, 1821–1922* (Princeton: Darwin Press, 1995).

——, *The Ottoman Peoples and the End of Empire* (Princeton: Darwin Press, 2001).

McDowall, David, *A Modern History of the Kurds* (London: I. B. Tauris, 2004).

Magdalino, Paul, *Studies on History and Topography of Byzantine Constantinople* (Aldershot: Ashgate, 2007).

Mansel, Philip, *Constantinople: City of the World's Desire, 1453–1924* (London: John Murray, 1995).

Meinecke, Michael, 'Die osmanische Architektur des 16. Jahrhunderts in Damaskus', *Fifth International Congress of Turkish Art* (Budapest: Akadémiai Kiadó, 1978), pp. 575–95.

——, *Patterns of Stylistic Change in Islamic Architecture: Local Traditions Versus Migrating Artists* (New York: New York University Press, 1996).

Melson, Robert, *Revolution and Genocide: On the Origins of the Armenian Genocide and Holocaust* (Chicago: University of Chicago Press, 1996).

Menemencioğlu, Nermin (ed.), *The Penguin Book of Turkish Verse* (Harmondsworth: Penguin, 1978).

Mikhail, Alan, *God's Shadow: The Ottoman Sultan Who Shaped the Modern World* (London: Faber & Faber, 2020).

Millner, Arthur, *Damascus Tiles: Mamluk and Ottoman Architectural Ceramics from Syria* (Munich/London/New York: Prestel, 2015).

Necipoğlu, Gülru, *The Age of Sinan: Architectural Culture in the Ottoman Empire* (London: Reaktion, 2005).

——, 'Anatolia and the Ottoman Legacy', in Martin Frishman and Hasan-Uddin Khan (eds.), *The Mosque: History, Architectural Development and Regional Diversity* (London: Thames & Hudson, 2002), pp. 141–57.

——, 'Challenging the Past: Sinan and the Competitive Discourse of Early Modern Islamic Architecture', *Muqarnas*, vol. 10 (1993), pp. 169–80.

——, 'Geometric Design in Timurid/Turkmen Architectural Practice: Thoughts on a Recently Discovered Scroll and Its Late Gothic Parallels', in Lisa Golombek and Maria Subtelny (eds.), *Timurid Art and Culture: Iran and Central Asia in the Fifteenth Century* (Leiden: E. J. Brill), 1992.

Ozturk, Ahmet Erdi, *Religion, Identity and Power: Turkey and the Balkans in the Twenty-First Century* (Edinburgh: Edinburgh University Press, 2021).

Pascual, Jean-Paul, *Damas à la fin du XVIe siècle* (Damascus: Institut Français de Damas, 1983).

——, 'Die Takkiya von Damaskus', in Mamoun Fansa, Heinz Gaube and Jens Windelberg (eds.), *Damaskus-Aleppo, 5000 Jahre Stadtentwicklung in Syrien* (Oldenburg: Isensee, 2000), pp. 271–76.

Pasinli, Alpay, and Saliha Balaman, *Turkish Tiles and Ceramics/Çinili Köşk* (Istanbul: Istanbul Archaeological Museums, 1991).

Peirce, Leslie, *Empress of the East: How a Slave Girl became Queen of the Ottoman Empire* (London: Icon Books, 2020).

Pennanen, R. P., 'The Nationalization of Ottoman Popular Music in Greece', *Ethnomusicology*, vol. 48, no. 1 (2004), pp. 1–25.

Porter, Venetia, *Islamic Tiles* (London: British Museum Press, 1995).

Quataert, Donald, *The Ottoman Empire, 1700–1922* (Cambridge: Cambridge University Press, 2000).

Renda, Günsel, and C. Max Kortepeter, *The Transformation of Turkish Culture: The Atatürk Legacy* (Princeton: Kingston Press, 1986).

Richter, Julius, *A History of Protestant Missions in the Near East* (Edinburgh: Oliphant, Anderson & Ferrier, 1910).

Rogan, Eugene, *The Fall of the Ottomans: The Great War in the Middle East, 1914–1920* (London, Penguin, 2015).

——, *Frontiers of the State in the Late Ottoman Empire* (Cambridge: Cambridge University Press, 1999).

Rogers, J. M., *Sinan* (London: I. B. Tauris, 2006).

Rozen, Minna, 'The Ottoman Jews', in *The Cambridge History of Turkey*, vol. 3: *The Later Ottoman Empire 1603–1839*, ed. Suraiya Faroqhi (Cambridge: Cambridge University Press, 2006), pp. 256–71.

Schamiloğlu, Uli, The Rise of the Ottoman Empire: The Black Death in Medieval Anatolia and Its Impact on Turkish Civilization', in Neguin Yavari et al. (eds.), *Views from the Edge: Essays in Honor of Richard W. Bulliet* (New York: Columbia University Press, 2004), pp. 255–79.

Schatkowski Schilcher, Linda, *Families in Politics: Damascene Factions and Estates of the 18th and 19th Centuries* (Stuttgart: Franz Steiner Verlag, 1985).

Shaw, Stanford J., and Ezel Kural Shaw, *History of the Ottoman Empire and Modern Turkey* (Cambridge: Cambridge University Press, 1977).

Shaw, Wendy, *Ottoman Painting: Reflections of Western Art from the Ottoman Empire to the Turkish Republic* (London: I. B. Tauris, 2001).

Teller, Matthew, *Nine Quarters of Jerusalem: A New Biography of the Old City* (London: Profile Books, 2022).

Thompson, Elizabeth, *Colonial Citizens: Republican Rights, Paternal Privilege, and Gender in French Syria and Lebanon* (New York: Columbia University Press, 2000).

Touma, Habib Hassan, 'Chapter 2: The Maqam Phenomenon', in *The Music of the Arabs*, trans. Laurie Schwarts (Portland, Ore., and Cambridge: Amadeus Press, 1996).

Varlık, Nükhet, *Plague and Empire in the Early Modern Mediterranean World: The Ottoman Experience 1347–1600* (Cambridge: Cambridge University Press, 2015).

Veinstein, Gilles (ed.), *Soliman le magnifique et son temps / Suleyman the Magnificent and his Time* (Paris: Ecole du Louvre, 1992).

Vogt-Goknil, Ulya, *Living Architecture: Ottoman* (London: Oldbourne, 1966).

Walker, Christopher J., *Armenia: The Survival of a Nation* (London: Croom Helm, 1980).

Weber, Stefan, 'The Creation of Ottoman Damascus: Architecture and Urban Development of Damascus in the 16th and 17th centuries', *ARAM*, vols. 9–10 (1997–98), pp. 431–70.

——, *Damascus: Ottoman Modernity and Urban Transformation, 1808–1918*, 2 vols. (Aarhus: Aarhus University Press, 2009).

——, 'Images of Imagined Worlds: Self-Image and Worldview in Late Ottoman Wall Paintings of Damascus', in Jens Hanssen, Thomas Philipp and Stefan Weber (eds.), *The Empire in the City: Arab Provincial Capitals in the Late Ottoman Empire* (Beirut: Orient-Institut der DMG Beirut, 2002).

Williams, Gwyn, *Eastern Turkey: A Guide and History* (London: Faber & Faber, 1972).

Yerasimos, Stephane, *Constantinople: Istanbul's Historical Heritage* (Königswinter: Tandem Verlag, 2007).

Yetkin, Şerare, *Historical Turkish Carpets*, trans. Maggie Quigley (Istanbul: Türkiye İş Bankası Cultural Publications, 1981).

Yetkin, Suut Kemal, 'The Evolution of Architectural Form in Turkish Mosques (1300–1700)', *Studia Islamica*, vol. 11 (1959), pp. 73–91.

Yılmaz, Şuhnaz, and Ipek K. Yoşmaoğlu, 'Fighting the Spectres of the Past: Dilemmas of Ottoman Legacy in the Balkans and the Middle East', *Middle Eastern Studies*, vol. 44, no. 5 (2008), pp. 677–93.

Yoltar-Yildirim, Ayşin, 'Raqqa: The Forgotten Excavation of an Islamic Site in Syria by the Ottoman Imperial Museum in the Early Twentieth Century', *Muqarnas*, vol. 30 (2013), pp. 73–93.

Zannos, Iannis, 'Intonation in Theory and Practice of Greek and Turkish Music', *Yearbook for Traditional Music*, vol. 22 (1990), pp. 42–59.

Zolberg, Aristide R., *State Formation and its Victims: Refugee Movements in Early Modern Europe* (Rotterdam: Erasmus University, 1982).

NOTES

INTRODUCTION
A Fresh View

1 Ian Almond, *Two Faiths, One Banner: When Muslims Marched with Christians across Europe's Battlegrounds* (London: I. B. Tauris, 2009), p. 140.
2 Warwick Ball, *Sultans of Rome: The Turkish World Expansion* (London: East and West Publishing, 2012), p. 93.
3 Ibid., p. 67.
4 Caroline Finkel, *Osman's Dream: The Story of the Ottoman Empire, 1300–1923* (London: John Murray, 2005), p. 11.
5 Anthony Bryer, 'Greek historians on the Turks: The case of the first Byzantine-Ottoman marriage', in R. Davis and J. Wallace Hadrill (eds.), *The Writing of History in the Middle Ages* (Oxford: Oxford University Press, 1981).
6 Ball, p. 147.

CHAPTER 1
The Ottoman Psyche

1 Doğan Kuban, *The Miracle of Divriği* (Istanbul: YKY, 2001), p. 173.
2 Ibid.
3 Heath Lowry, *The Nature of the Early Ottoman State* (New York: State University of New York Press, 2003), p. 43.
4 Caroline Finkel, *Osman's Dream: The Story of the Ottoman Empire 1300–1923* (London: John Murray, 2005), p. 9.
5 Warwick Ball, *Sultans of Rome: The Turkish World Expansion* (London: East and West Publishing, 2012), p. 110.

CHAPTER 2
The Commercial Spirit

1 Warwick Ball, *Sultans of Rome: The Turkish World Expansion* (London: East and West Publishing, 2012), p. 114.
2 Ibid.
3 'Bursa and Cumalıkızık: The Birth of the Ottoman Empire': https://whc.unesco.org/en/list/1452/ (accessed 22 November 2021).
4 Suraiya Faroqhi, *Travel and Artisans in the Ottoman Empire* (London: I. B. Tauris, 2014), p. 102.
5 Ibid., p. 103.
6 Ibid.
7 Ibid., p. 105.
8 Ibid., p. 212.
9 Ibid., p. 104.
10 Ibid., p. xix.
11 Leila T. Erder, 'The Making of Industrial Bursa', unpublished PhD thesis, Princeton University, 1976.
12 Haim Gerber, 'Social and Economic Position of Women in an Ottoman City: Bursa, 1600–1700', *International Journal of Middle East Studies*, vol. 12, no. 3 (1980), p. 237.
13 Faroqhi, p. 116.
14 Eugene Rogan, *Frontiers of the State in the Late Ottoman*

Empire (Cambridge: Cambridge University Press, 1999), p. 66.

15 Evliya Çelebi, *Seyahatname*, 10 vols. (Istanbul, 1896–1938).

16 Faroqhi, p. xi.

17 Ibid.

18 Ibid.

19 See Jonathan Gathorne-Hardy, *The Sultan's Organ* (Norwich: Propolis, 2017).

20 Stefan Weber, *Damascus: Ottoman Modernity and Urban Transformation, 1808–1918*, 2 vols. (Aarhus: Aarhus University Press, 2009).

21 Doğan Kuban, *The Turkish Hayat House* (Istanbul: Eren, 1995), p. 235.

22 'Masterpieces from the V&A in Damascus': https://funci.org/masterpieces-from-the-va-in-damascus/?lang=en (accessed 8 October 2021).

23 Halil Inalcık and Donald Quataert (eds.), *An Economic and Social History of the Ottoman Empire, 1300–1919* (Cambridge: Cambridge University Press, 1994), p. 4.

CHAPTER 3
Statecraft and Geography

1 Warwick Ball, *Sultans of Rome: The Turkish World Expansion* (London: East and West Publishing, 2012), p. 95.

2 Caroline Finkel, *Osman's Dream: The Story of the Ottoman Empire 1300–1923* (London: John Murray, 2005), p. 310.

3 Ibid., p. 97.

4 Finkel, p. 16.

5 Cited in Ball, p. 102.

6 Cited in Ball, p. 117.

7 Gülru Necipoğlu, *The Age of Sinan: Architectural Culture in the Ottoman Empire* (London: Reaktion, 2005), p. 88.

8 Cited in Ball, p. 114.

9 Giancarlo Casale, *The Ottoman Age of Exploration* (New York and Oxford: Oxford University Press, 2010), pp. 39–40.

10 Philip Mansel, *Constantinople: City of the World's Desire, 1453–1924* (London: John Murray, 1995), p. 18.

11 Ball, p. 112.

12 Donald Quataert, *The Ottoman Empire, 1700–1922* (Cambridge: Cambridge University Press, 2000), p. 136.

13 Ball, p. 113.

14 Dawn Chatty, *Syria: The Making and Unmaking of a Refuge State* (London: Hurst, 2017), p. 18.

15 Ibid., p. 19.

16 Quoted in Mansel, p. 15.

17 https://www.irishcentral.com/roots/history/generous-turkish-aid-irish-great-hunger (accessed 11 October 2021).

18 Chatty, p. 29.

19 Justin McCarthy, *The Ottoman Peoples and the End of Empire* (Princeton: Darwin Press, 2001), p. 21.

20 Quataert, p. 652.

21 Stanford J. Shaw and Ezel Kural Shaw, *History of the Ottoman Empire and Modern Turkey* (Cambridge: Cambridge University Press, 1977), vol. 2, p. 115.

22 Ibid., p. 116.

23 Tharik Hussain, *Minarets in the Mountains* (Chesham: Bradt Guides, 2021), pp. 56–58.

24 R. Stephen Humphreys, *Between Memory and Desire: The Middle East in a Troubled Age* (Berkeley: University of California Press, 1999).

25 Chatty, p. 39.

CHAPTER 4
Religious Values

1 See Caroline Finkel, *Osman's Dream: The Story of the Ottoman Empire 1300–1923* (London: John Murray, 2005), p. 8.

2 Rudi Lindner, *Nomads and Ottomans in Medieval Anatolia* (Bloomington, Ind.: Indiana University, 1983), p. 37.

3 Warwick Ball, *Sultans of Rome: The Turkish World Expansion* (London: East and West Publishing, 2012), p. 123.

4 Ibid., p. 124.

5 Finkel, p. 10.

6 Ibid., p. 9.

7 Doğan Kuban, *The Miracle of Divriği* (Istanbul: YKY, 2001), p. 93.

8 Finkel, p. 10.

9 Ball, p. 93.

10 Patrick Kinross, *The Ottoman Centuries: The Rise and Fall of the Turkish Empire* (New York: Morrow, 1977), p. 40.

11 Norman Stone, 'Forget the Holy War Theory', *Cornucopia*, vol. 29, no. 5 (2003), pp. 26–28.

12 Ian Almond, *Two Faiths, One Banner: When Muslims Marched with Christians across Europe's Battlegrounds* (London: I. B. Tauris, 2009), pp. 151–53.

13 Finkel, pp. 18–19.

14 See Carole Hillenbrand, *Turkish Myth and Muslim Symbol: The Battle of Manzikert* (Edinburgh: Edinburgh University Press, 2007), pp. 172–77.

15 Dawn Chatty, *Syria: The Making and Unmaking of a Refuge State* (London: Hurst, 2017), p. 23.

16 Ibid., p. 24.

17 Ibid., p. 25.

18 Ibid., p. 27.

19 Ziya Enver Karal, 'Non-Muslim Representatives in the First Constitutional Assembly, 1876–1877', in Benjamin Braude and Bernard Lewis (eds.), *Christians and Jews in the Ottoman Empire* (New York: Holmes & Meier 1982), p. 388.

20 Chatty, p. 27.

21 Ball, p. 116.

22 Ibid., p. 120.

23 Ibid., p. 119.

24 Tharik Hussain, *Minarets in the Mountains* (Chesham: Bradt Guides, 2021), pp. 227, 234.

25 Ibid., p. 167.

26 https://whc.unesco.org/en/tentativelists/5735/ (accessed 13 October 2021).

CHAPTER 5
Scientific and Industrial Innovations

1 See L. Carl Brown (ed.), *Imperial Legacy: The Ottoman Imprint on the Balkans and the Middle East* (New York: Columbia University Press, 1996), p. 248.

2 Salim Ayduz and Huseyin Sen, 'Taqī al-Dīn ibn Marūf', in *The Oxford Encyclopedia of Philosophy, Science, and Technology in Islam: Oxford Islamic Studies Online*: http://www.oxfordislamicstudies.com/article/opr/t445/e231 (accessed 14 October 2021).

3 Halil Inalcık, 'Learning, the Medrese, and the Ulema', in *The Ottoman Empire: The Classical Age, 1300–1600* (New York: Praeger, 1973), pp. 165–78.

4 Lucy Mary Jane Garnett, *Turkish Life in Town and Country* (New York: G. P. Putnam's Sons, 1904), p. 196.

5 Jerry Brotton, *Trading Territories: Mapping the Early Modern World* (London: Reaktion, 2003), p. 109.

6 *Hezarfen* is Persian for 'a thousand sciences'.

7 Evliya Çelebi, *Seyahatname*, ed. Seyit Ali Kahraman, Yücel Dağlı and Robert Dankoff (Istanbul: YKY, 2003), vol. 8, p. 318.

8 Evliya Çelebi, quoted in Frank H. Winter, 'Who First Flew in a Rocket?', *Journal of the British Interplanetary Society*, no. 45 (July 1992), pp. 275–80.

9 Information taken from Donald Quaetert and Ryan Gingeras, 'Miners and the State in the Ottoman Empire' (2008), on *Ottoman History Podcast*: https://www.ottomanhistorypodcast.com/2014/05/miners-turkey-ottoman-empire.html (accessed 14 October 2021).

CHAPTER 6
Literary Curiosities

1 Geoffrey Lewis, 'The Ottoman Legacy in Language', in L. Carl Brown (ed.), *Imperial Legacy: The Ottoman Imprint on the Balkans and the Middle East* (New York: Columbia University Press, 1996), p. 214.

2 Ibid., p. 216.

3 Geoffrey Lewis (ed. and trans.), *The Book of Dede Korkut* (Harmondsworth: Penguin, 1974), p. 9.

4 Ibid., p. 10.

5 James Kritzeck (ed.), *Anthology of Islamic Literature* (Harmondsworth: Penguin, 1964), p. 389.

6 Ibid., p. 380.

7 Ibid., p. 374.

8 Charles F. Horne (ed.), *The Sacred Books and Early Literature of the East* (New York: Parke, Austin, & Lipscomb, 1917), vol. 6: *Medieval Arabia*, p. 259: https://sourcebooks.fordham.edu/source/turkishpoetry1.asp (accessed 18 October 2021).

9 The name Rumi means 'the one from Rum', i.e. the Seljuk sultanate whose capital was Konya.

10 Nermin Menemencioğlu (ed.), *The Penguin Book of Turkish Verse* (Harmondsworth: Penguin, 1978), p. 88.

11 Leslie Peirce, *Empress of the East: How a Slave Girl became Queen of the Ottoman Empire* (London: Icon Books, 2020), p. 155.

12 Islamic and Indian Art sale, 24 April 2018, lot 93: https://www.bonhams.com/auctions/24623/lot/93/?category=list (accessed 18 October 2021).

13 Alan Mikhail, *God's Shadow: The Ottoman Sultan Who Shaped the Modern World* (London: Faber & Faber, 2020), p. 334.

14 https://sites.google.com/site/1000objectsbritishmuseum/home/tughra-of-suleiman-the-magnificent (accessed 18 October 2021).

15 Peirce, pp. 154–55.

16 Kritzeck, p. 234.

17 https://day.kyiv.ua/en/article/culture/one-remembered-five-centuries-end (accessed 18 October 2021).

18 Information taken from Leslie Peirce, 'Hürren Sultan or Roxelana, Empress of the East' (2017), on *Ottoman History Podcast*: https://www.ottomanhistorypodcast.com/2017/12/roxelana.html (accessed 22 November 2021).

19 https://www.nytimes.com/2011/03/17/world/middleeast/17iht-m17-soap.html (accessed 18 October 2021).

20 Menemencioğlu, p. 92.

21 Chris Gratien and Didem Havlioğlu, 'Love Poems of an Ottoman Woman: Mihrî Hatun' (2018), a podcast on *Ottoman History*: https://www.ottomanhistorypodcast.com/2018/04/mihri-hatun.html (accessed 19 October 2021).

22 See Giancarlo Casale (ed. and trans.), *Prisoner of the Infidels: The Memoir of an Ottoman Muslim in Seventeenth-Century Europe* (Berkeley: University of California Press, 2021).

CHAPTER 7
Musical Traditions

1 Carl Engel, *Researches into the Early History of the Violin Family* (Amsterdam: Antiqua, 1965), p. 79.

2 https://day.kyiv.ua/en/article/culture/one-remembered-five-centuries-end (accessed 19 October 2021).

3 Iannis Zannos, 'Intonation in Theory and Practice of Greek and Turkish Music', *Yearbook for Traditional Music*, vol. 22 (1990), pp. 42–59.

4 See R. P. Pennanen, 'The Nationalization of Ottoman Popular Music in Greece', *Ethnomusicology*, vol. 48, no. 1 (2004), pp. 1–25.

CHAPTER 8
Medical Mores

1 Elias John Wilkinson Gibb, *A History of Ottoman Poetry*, 6 vols. (London: Luzac, 1958–67).

2 Robert Dankoff and Sooyong Kim, *An Ottoman Traveller: Selections from the Book of Travels of Evliya Çelebi* (London: Eland, 2011), p. 247.

3 Osman Şevki Uludağ, *Beş Buçuk Asırlık Türk Tababet Tarihi* (Five and a Half Centuries of Turkish Medical History) (Istanbul, 1969), pp. 35–36.

4 Nükhet Varlık, *Plague and Empire in the Early Modern Mediterranean World: The Ottoman Experience 1347–1600* (Cambridge: Cambridge University Press, 2015).

5 Ibid., p. 256.

6 See e.g. Yaron Ayalon, 'The Black Death and the Rise of the Ottomans', in *Natural Disasters in the Ottoman Empire* (Cambridge: Cambridge University Press, 2014).

7 Letter 36, to Mrs S. C. from Adrianople (n.d.): Lady Mary Wortley Montagu, *Letters of the Right Honourable Lady M--y W--y M--e: Written During her Travels in Europe, Asia and Africa*, vol. 1 (Aix: Anthony Henricy, 1796), pp. 167–69.

8 Didem Tali, 'A New Deal for Turkey's Homeless Dogs', *New York Times*, 2 October 2019.

CHAPTER 9
Aesthetic Sensitivities

1 https://en.wikipedia.org/wiki/DOBAG_Carpet_Initiative (accessed 21 October 2021).

2 S. H. Nasr (ed. and trans.), *Epistles of the Brethren of Purity* (Beirut: Dar Sadir, 1957), vol. 1, p. 37.

3 Doğan Kuban, *The Miracle of Divriği* (Istanbul: YKY, 2001), p. 178.

4 Arthur Millner, *Damascus Tiles: Mamluk and Ottoman Architectural Ceramics from Syria* (Munich/London/New York: Prestel, 2015), p. 113.

5 Gülru Necipoğlu, *The Age of Sinan: Architectural Culture in the Ottoman Empire* (London: Reaktion, 2005), p. 495.

6 Ibid., p. 220.

7 Ibid., p. 107.

8 Ibid., p. 106.

9 Evliya Çelebi, *Seyahatname*, 10 vols. (Istanbul, 1896–1938), vol. 1, p. 152.

10 Necipoğlu, p. 107.

11 Ibid.

CHAPTER 10
Architectural Identity

1 Doğan Kuban, *The Miracle of Divriği* (Istanbul: YKY, 2001), p. 97.

2 G. Lechler, 'The Tree of Life in Indo-European and Islamic Cultures', *Ars Islamica*, vol. 4 (1937), p. 380.

3 Gülru Necipoğlu, *The Age of Sinan: Architectural Culture in the Ottoman Empire* (London: Reaktion, 2005), p. 84.

4 Ibid., p. 154.

5 Ibid, p. 114.

6 Ulya Vogt-Göknil, *Living Architecture: Ottoman* (London: Oldbourne, 1966), p. 146.

7 Stephane Yerasimos, *Constantinople: Istanbul's Historical Heritage* (Königswinter: Tandem Verlag, 2007), p. 297.

8 Necipoğlu, p. 150.

9 A mystic miracle-working saint; 'al-Khidr' in Arabic, meaning 'the Green One' (sometimes associated with St George).

10 Necipoğlu, p. 147.

11 Ibid., p. 426.
12 Ibid., p. 215.
13 Ibid.
14 Ibid., p. 150.
15 https://whc.unesco.org/
en/list/1366/ (accessed
22 November 2021).
16 Alpay Pasinli and Saliha
Balaman, *Turkish Tiles and
Ceramics/Çinili Köşk* (Istanbul:
Istanbul Archaeological
Museums, 1991), p. 28.
17 Information taken from Hakan
Tarhan, 'Public Perceptions of
the Other's Heritage: Ottoman
Heritage in Greece' (online
lecture, British Institute, Ankara,
8 June 2021).
18 Jacques de Villamont, *Les
Voyages* (Paris, 1606), p. 435.
19 One of the leading festivals in
the Middle East, it was launched
in 1984 in defiance of the war,
hosting such stars as Plácido
Domingo, Fairuz and Elton John.
20 An exhibition entitled 'Alpaslan
Ataman – Timeless Architecture'
was held at the GAD Gallery in
Nişantaşi, Turkey, in 2021.

CHAPTER 11
Culinary Delights

1 Robert Dankoff and Sooyong
Kim, *An Ottoman Traveller:
Selections from the Book of
Travels of Evliya Çelebi* (London:
Eland, 2011), pp. 246–47.
2 Doğan Kuban, *Ottoman
Architecture* (Woodbridge:
Antique Collectors Club, 2010),
p. 415.
3 https://www.theguardian.
com/lifeandstyle/
wordofmouth/2010/sep/21/
consider-sherbet (accessed
25 October 2021).
4 Warwick Ball, *Sultans of Rome:
The Turkish World Expansion*
(London: East and West
Publishing, 2012), p. 146.
5 Markman Ellis, *The Coffee
House: A Cultural History*
(London: Weidenfeld &
Nicolson, 2011), p. 67.
6 James Kritzeck (ed.),
Anthology of Islamic Literature
(Harmondsworth: Penguin,
1964), p. 387.
7 Ibrahim Peçevi, quoted in
Bernard Lewis, *Istanbul and
the Civilization of the Ottoman
Empire* (Norman, Okla.:
University of Oklahoma Press,
1963), p. 132.
8 Ivo Andrić, *The Bridge over
the Drina* [1945], trans. Lovett
F. Edwards (London: Harvill,
1994), p. 15.
9 Evliya Çelebi, *Seyahatname*, 10
vols. (Istanbul, 1896–1938), vol. 1.
10 Nermin Menemencioğlu (ed.),
*The Penguin Book of Turkish
Verse* (Harmondsworth:
Penguin, 1978), p. 205.

CHAPTER 12
Home and Lifestyle

1 See Doğan Kuban, *The Turkish
Hayat House* (Istanbul: Eren,
1995).
2 https://whc.unesco.org/
en/list/614/ (accessed
22 November 2021).

3 https://whc.unesco.org/en/list/569/ (accessed 22 November 2021).

4 The Ottomans kept meticulous records for all their provinces in the form of 'yearbooks'. These provide a wealth of information for historians and researchers today.

5 Held in the Topkapı Palace Museum, this album was a collection of thirty-two paintings, drawings and examples of calligraphy assembled in 1610 for Sultan Ahmet I (r. 1603–17). It earned its compiler, an Ottoman bureaucrat and courtier called Kalender Pasha (d. 1616), a promotion and serves as an intriguing example of Ottoman artistic patronage.

6 Amelia Soth, 'The Movable Tent Cities of the Ottoman Empire' (4 July 2019), on the *JSTOR Daily* website: https://daily.jstor.org/the-movable-tent-cities-of-the-ottoman-empire/ (accessed 22 November 2021).

7 Amy Singer, 'Enter, Riding on an Elephant: How to Approach Early Ottoman Edirne', *Journal of the Ottoman and Turkish Studies Association*, vol. 3, no. 1 (May 2016), p. 104.

8 See Sinem Erdoğan Işkorkutan, *The 1720 Imperial Circumcision Celebrations in Istanbul* (Leiden: Brill, 2020).

CONCLUSION
Lessons for the Future?

1 Mark Mazower, *The Balkans: From the End of Byzantium to the Present Day* (London, Weidenfeld & Nicolson, 2000), p. 4.

2 Ibid., p. 2.

3 Jessica Bateman, 'Coming home after 130 years', *BBC News* website: https://www.bbc.co.uk/news/stories-44242621 (accessed 8 November 2021).

4 Keith Hitchens, *A Concise History of Romania* (Cambridge: Cambridge University Press, 2014), p. 61.

5 Giancarlo Casale (ed. and trans.), *Prisoner of the Infidels: The Memoir of an Ottoman Muslim in Seventeenth-Century Europe* (Berkeley: University of California Press, 2021).

SOURCES OF ILLUSTRATIONS

INDEX